THE NFT HANDBOOK FOR BEGINNERS

THE COMPLETE CRASH COURSE TO CREATING,
SELLING, AND BUYING NON-FUNGIBLE TOKENS -
MAKE MONEY USING CRYPTOCURRENCY AND
BLOCKCHAIN TECHNOLOGY

BRETT GARLAND

CONTENTS

Introduction   9

1. BLOCKCHAIN TECHNOLOGY   17
   What Is a Blockchain?   17
   How Does It Work?   19
   History of Blockchain Technology   20
   Benefits and Drawbacks of Blockchain
   Technology   23

2. CRYPTOCURRENCY   31
   What Is Cryptocurrency?   31
   Key Concepts of Cryptocurrency   32
   How Does Cryptocurrency Work?   34
   Where Do Cryptocurrencies Get Their
   Value?   37
   How to Use Cryptocurrency for Secure
   Purchases   38
   How to Invest in Cryptocurrency   39
   Should You Invest in Cryptocurrency?   40
   Why Is Cryptocurrency the Future of
   Finance?   41

3. CRYPTO MINING   43
   What Is Crypto Mining?   43
   Mining Computers, Rigs, and Farms   44
   Who Updates the Blockchain and How
   Frequently?   49
   How Does Bitcoin Mining Work?   50
   Reasons Why Bitcoin Needs Miners   51
   How to Start Mining Bitcoin   52

If Cryptocurrency Mining Is So Simple,
Why Doesn't Everyone Do It?   54
Crypto Mining Games & Simulators   58

4. NON-FUNGIBLE TOKENS (NFTS)   61
What Makes NFTs Unique?   63
Why Do People Buy NFTs?   66
Why Do Some Avoid NFTs?   68
According to the Experts   69
The Possibilities of NFTs   73
The Value of NFTs   78
What About Physical Items?   80
Smart Contracts   80

5. THE ETHEREUM VIRTUAL MACHINE   85
Defining Ethereum Virtual Machine   86
The Purpose of the Ethereum Virtual
Machine   86
Benefits of Ethereum Virtual Machine   87
Downsides of the Ethereum Virtual
Machine   88
What Is Turing-Completeness?   89
Ethereum Virtual Machine Features   90
The EVM Economy   94
How Does the Ethereum Virtual Machine
Work?   95
What Is Ethereum Gas?   97
The Significance of the Ethereum Virtual
Machine   98
Ethereum 2.0—The Future of the EVM   99

6. NFT MARKETPLACES   101
Choosing an NFT Marketplace   101
Popular NFT Marketplaces   105

7. NON-FUNGIBLE GOODWILL   115

8. CRYPTO WALLETS 119
What Are Crypto Wallets? 119
Understanding How Crypto Wallets
Work 120
Types of Crypto Wallets 122
How Do You Create a Cryptocurrency
Wallet 126
Getting Started With Coinbase 130
How to Quickly Earn $17 For FREE—No
Strings Attached! 134
Crypto Wallet Considerations 136

9. A KICKSTART GUIDE TO INVESTING
IN NFTS 139
Should You Buy NFTs? 140
Are NFTs an Ideal Investment for You? 142
Steps to Invest in NFT 142
FAQs 145

10. INCOME WITH NFTS 147
Passive Income 148
Active Income 151

11. CREATE, BUY, AND SELL NFTS 155
Creating NFTs 156
Selling Your NFT 158
Buying NFTs on OpenSea 158
Selling Your NFT on OpenSea 160

12. POTENTIAL RISKS 163
Smart Contract Risks and Maintenance
of NFTs 164
Legal Challenges 164
Cyber Threats and Online Fraud Risks 165
Intellectual Property Rights 165
Valuation Challenges 166
NFTs as Securities Challenges 166

What Are the Experts Saying About the
Risks?   167
Can These Risks be Mitigated?   171

13. NFTS AND TAXES   173
    Are NFTs Taxable?   173
    IRS and NFTs   177

14. THE METAVERSE   179
    What Is the Metaverse?   179
    The Origins of the Metaverse   180
    How Does Crypto Fit Into the Metaverse?   181
    Metaverse Examples   184
    Web 3.0 vs. the Metaverse: What's the
    Difference?   186
    Future of the Metaverse   190

    Conclusion   193
    References   195

This book is dedicated to JC, IG, and GG, for all that you have vested in me.

INTRODUCTION

"Every person who is fortunate enough to live in the next 15 years will have many digital possessions. NFTs will be seen as a new form of identification, social money, and brand recognition."

— GARY VAYNERCHUK

What's the big deal about owning something you can't physically hold in your hands? Aren't NFTs and cryptocurrencies new, volatile, and challenging to regulate? Yes. But that is precisely why so many people are diving into this new space. Although, the seemingly unimaginable profits are part of the allure as well.

You may or may not believe in NFTs, but if you are reading this book, you're at least curious about their potential. After all, when it comes to money, you should never put all your eggs in one basket. Wise investors know they need to diversify to protect their hard-earned cash. Of course, it also helps to have the odds in your favor. In the following chapters, you'll read about several creators and sellers who just happened to be in the right place at the right time.

A BRIEF HISTORY

Before we look at the ins and outs of NFTs and blockchain technology, let us look at the history of this ever-growing phenomenon.

2012-2013: Colored Coins

In 2012-2013, the Bitcoin blockchain introduced the colored coin, which paved the way for the emergence of NFTs. Colored coins are tokens that act as real-world assets on the blockchain and can prove ownership of cars, real estate, precious metals, bonds, and equities (Wong, 2021). This new technology provided a glimpse into the possibilities of tokenization.

2014: Counterparty

Counterparty is an open-sourced, peer-to-peer financial platform launched in 2014 (Wong, 2021). Founded by Robert Dermody, Evan Wagner, and Adam Krellenstein on the Bitcoin blockchain, it allows users to create and use their tradable currencies on a decentralized exchange.

2015: Spells of Genesis on Counterparty

In 2015, Counterparty pioneered the use of in-game assets via blockchain with the makers of the game Spells of Genesis (Steinwold, 2019). They were one of the first to launch an Initial Coin Offering (ICO) to raise funds for their startup. They helped finance Counterparty's development by establishing BitCrystals (an in-game currency).

2016: Trading Cards on Counterparty

In August 2016, Counterparty partnered with Force of Will, a popular trading card game, and turned these into trading cards available on their platform. In North America, Force of Will ranked fourth behind Pokemon, Yu-Gi-Oh, and Magic: The Gathering trading cards in terms of sales volume (Steinwold, 2019). This collection and its success proved the value of putting these kind of assets on a blockchain.

2016-2017: Rare Pepe

In October 2016, memes entered the blockchain and began permeating the Counterparty platform. People could add assets made from a particular meme— Pepe the Frog— which featured an intriguing frog character and had accumulated a large fan base. Pepe the Frog became an internet sensation and one of the most iconic memes of its time that it even has its own directory for trading "Rare Pepes" on a Rare Pepe Directory (Steinwold, 2019). Things started to shift in early 2017, and Rare Pepe NFTs began to be traded on the Ethereum blockchain.

2017: CryptoPunks

As Rare Pepe trading picked up steam in 2017, Larva Labs creators John Watkinson and Matt Hall created a set of 8-bit characters with unique, identifying features. To develop a feeling of exclusivity, they only minted a specific number of images (10,000). Thus introducing the concept of scarcity to the NFT world.

CryptoPunks - Example of Aliens

These pixelated images of humans, zombies, apes, and aliens (the rarest of all) display a unique combination of 87 attributes (Thomas, 2022).

2018: CryptoKitties

CryptoKitties took off in 2018 on the Ethereum blockchain. It is a virtual game that allows players to adopt, breed, and trade cats using Ethereum cryptocurrency. The project went viral soon after the company Axiom Zen introduced it to developers at a major coding event called a hackathon (Wolfsen, 2018). The game made headlines on CNBC and Fox News, turning the public's attention to NFTs.

2018-2020: NFT Gaming

NFTs slowly but surely caught the attention of the gaming industry. Games that allowed tokenization of in-game assets began to surface. The first virtual reality (VR) decentralized Ethereum-based platform was Decentraland (MANA). Gamers could explore the virtual world, build on land they owned, play games, and collect in-game items. Following that, other games like Axie Infinity (AXS) developed on the blockchain. This battle and trading game is partially owned and operated by its community of players.

2021: The NFT Explosion

The interest in NFTs increased in 2021, and other blockchains like Solana, Tezos, Cardano, and Flow began releasing their version of tokens. With new standards established to ensure that NFTs were authentic and unique, there was a surge in NFT purchases at the beginning of the second quarter. Although many people thought the NFT bubble would burst, assets grew in the fourth quarter, especially when Facebook announced that its parent company would rebrand to Meta with plans to join the metaverse soon (Butler, 2021).

THIS BOOK

As NFTs become popular in the coming years, investors have different reasons for jumping on the bandwagon. Like physical art, people collect NFTs for the value and the recognition they bring. Some people find it hard to understand how to invest in such a different type of asset. NFTs are a complete paradigm shift—one that is unregulated. Their biggest fear is that NFTs are merely a transitory fad that will soon disappear. Despite all this, investors are terrified of missing out on good investment opportunities because of the hype surrounding them.

With any kind of investing, it pays to be cautious. Many projects may have started with a bang but die out soon after. It is essential to educate yourself and do your research before investing in anything that catches your eye. I have prepared a handy guide with informative facts to help you decide whether to join the digital wave or pass on the enormous opportunity. Reading this book will start you on your journey by educating you on everything NFT-related. You will get the most up-to-date and verified knowledge regarding NFTs.

This book is an eye-opener for retail investors willing to dip their toes into new waters. It will give you access to a constantly growing and expanding world and introduce you to the concepts of the metaverse and web 3.0. In short, this book will guide you on how to make money while navigating the space as a creator, seller, or long-term investor. The following few chapters are a good starting point for anyone wanting a solid grasp of NFTs, cryptocurrencies, and blockchain technology, including how to invest and mine crypto, prepare for taxes, and so much more!

If you are curious about the world of NFTs, read on ...

1

BLOCKCHAIN TECHNOLOGY

WHAT IS A BLOCKCHAIN?

To understand NFTs, cryptocurrency, and smart contracts, you must first understand what a blockchain is. Blockchain technology is one of the most decisive technological innovations of our time. It has shaped how digital transactions are verified and stored. Using Distributed Ledger Technology (DLT), the blockchain is simply a decentralized ledger that records where transactions originate (also known as provenance) and prevents tampering or manipulation by outside sources. This makes it a legitimate and trustworthy medium when making digital transactions (*Blockchain, n.d.*). On the blockchain, each transaction is permanent and tamper-proof.

Using cryptographic *hashing* (like a digital key or fingerprint) and decentralization, information is distributed simultaneously instead of being transferred or copied. This provides real-time access to transactions within the blockchain. Let's use Google Docs as an example. When the document is created and shared with a group of people, it's not copied nor transferred but distributed (*Blockchain*, n.d.). All changes are made and recorded in real-time for everyone to see. The same is true for transactions on the blockchain. Users can see what was done and when—at any time. This is the beauty of a decentralized ledger.

People use blockchain technology in cryptocurrency, healthcare, cyber security, bill pay, and games. It brings transparency in a scalable and desirable way that ensures users are not getting scammed.

HOW DOES IT WORK?

Blockchains have three essential concepts: blocks, miners, and nodes.

Blocks: Blocks contain the data and are labeled with a random, 32-bit whole number (called a nonce). The nonce, in turn, generates a hash, which serves as the block's unique signature.

Miners: Through "mining," the miners create new blocks on the chain. They use specific software and advanced hardware to solve mathematical problems that result in the nonce (that generates the hash). Every participating miner is given a unique alphanumeric identifier that shows their transactions in the blockchain. Mining a block requires lots of time and computing power. Therefore, miners are rewarded every time they successfully manage to mine a block. These rewards compensate for the time and facilities spent during the mining process.

Nodes: Nodes keep the entire blockchain distributed and updated. Every existing node has a copy of the blockchain, and the network of nodes must approve any newly-mined block for the chain to be trusted, verified, and updated.

HISTORY OF BLOCKCHAIN TECHNOLOGY

Unknown to many, the advent of blockchain technology started in the early 1990s. It was one of the most significant innovations of the 21st century. The utilization of the blockchain impacted many industries, including manufacturing, financial sectors, and even education (Iredale, 2020). Many apps soon followed because of the blockchain's popularity, attempting to vie for a piece of the pie as digital economies expanded.

1991-2008: Blockchain's Infancy

In 1991, W. Scott Stornetta and Stuart Haber first introduced the technology behind the blockchain. They worked to develop a cryptographically secured chain of blocks where no one could manipulate the timestamp of documents. A year later, they upgraded the system to include Merkle trees (a data structure that uses leaf-nodes to verify and sync data) to enhance efficiency, enabling one block to collect more records than before.

Seventeen years later, Satoshi Nakamoto created the first application ever used on decentralized ledger technology (DLT)—Bitcoin. In a detailed report published in 2009 (referred to as a whitepaper), he explained that the technology could enhance digital trust due to its decentralized nature and outlined how it prevented any entity from being in total control of anything (Iredale,

2020). Although Nakamoto is recognized as the brains behind blockchain technology, their true identity remains unknown.

Since then, Nakamoto has vanished but handed over the development of Bitcoin to other core developers resulting in new applications other than cryptocurrencies that make up the blockchain story as we know it today.

2008-2013: A Bit of Coin Emerges

While many believe Bitcoin and Blockchain are equivalent, this is not the case. Simply put, Bitcoin is a cryptocurrency powered by blockchain technology. In 2010, Bitcoins could be mined using a personal computer. And on May 22, the first public transaction for Bitcoin was made when two pizzas were purchased for 10,000BTC.

2013-2015: A Smarter Ether Develops

Vitalik Buterin, a software developer and one of the first contributors to the Bitcoin codebase, felt that Bitcoin lacked something important. So, in 2013, he began working on a blockchain that could function in various ways aside from simply being a peer-to-peer network. As a result, smart contracts emerged.

Smart contracts were impossible to integrate within Bitcoin's blockchain without compromising the blockchain itself because it had already been established. This gave rise to a new blockchain called Ethereum. Smart contracts allow users on new blockchains (like Ethereum) to perform more tasks than just monitoring cryptocurrency.

Since its launch in 2015, Ethereum has gathered a large following, giving it a reputable name among existing cryptocurrencies (Iredale, 2020). Due to its functionality, it is now second to Bitcoin in terms of usage. We will talk more about Ethereum and smart contracts later.

2018-2021: Blockchain Growth

Blockchain innovation did not end with the rise of Bitcoin and Ethereum. Quite a few projects integrated innovative blockchain technology over the next few years. Some companies began to leverage the capabilities of the new technology and address the issues that previous blockchains could not. These include scalability, security, and decentralization.

Although China has banned numerous cryptocurrencies, it remained active and up to date regarding blockchain technology. Some of these applications included NEO, which was said to be the first decentralized, open-source, and blockchain platform in China. In addition, NEO addressed some of the scalability issues with the initial Bitcoin blockchain.

Aside from NEO, other second-generation blockchain platforms addressed some scalability and security issues, which gave rise to altcoins such as Monero, ZCash, and Dash. Even companies like Microsoft and Apple started taking an interest in blockchain applications.

2022-Present: To Infinity...and Beyond

Today, the future of blockchain looks bright and promising, given that the whole world is finally paying attention. Advocates expect blockchain technology to automate most, if not all, of the tasks done by professionals in all sectors. This brings hope of saving considerable time, money, and human resources.

BENEFITS AND DRAWBACKS OF BLOCKCHAIN TECHNOLOGY

Blockchain technology was initially portrayed as a groundbreaking technology that provided unprecedented levels of security—something not only IT and financial industries wanted but all industries in general, making it a very adaptable technology (Frizzo-Barker et al., 2020). When compared to standard database systems, the blockchain is a superior technology. Furthermore, no single company may control the blockchain, so there is no risk of exploitation or censorship from any party.

Despite its many advantages, Blockchain technology is far from flawless; its deployment has benefits and drawbacks, much like any revolutionary technology. Let's explore a few of them.

Benefits

The technology is decentralized. This technology is more secure than centralized systems because of its distribution across a vast network of computers that operate within the same platform and never with a standalone server or computer. So if someone tampers with an existing record, they will immediately be seen by others within the network.

Blockchain transactions are transparent. Once someone successfully makes a transaction, miners create ledgers inside the platform for everyone to see. The public will see the client's wallet address and the wallet's balance even if they cannot identify who the client is. This digital ledger, distributed across the network, helps prevent fraud.

It has improved confidentiality. Blockchain users can choose whether or not to put their names and addresses on their transactions or remain anonymous, providing another layer of security. This also prevents sites from targeting you with location-based ads.

Blockchain transactions are more secure. For hackers to access blockchains, they need to hack every block inside the chain to seize control. Each block has a password that can be up to one hundred characters. It would take them years, or even decades, to open a single block. Hence, blockchain-based applications are reliable and secure.

Transactions are processed faster. You do not need a third party or mediator to make transactions inside the blockchain. Because of the peer-to-peer network system, transactions are more straightforward and faster compared to traditional banks, their fees and transfers.

Its operating costs are low. Blockchains do not need servers, mediators, or go-betweens to function since there is no centralized authority, drastically reducing overhead costs. They also eliminate the need for third-party services such as merchants and banks, cutting out the processing time and banking fees.

Blockchains provide better accessibility. Unlike banks and other financial services, people can take advantage of the blockchain regardless of their financial situation or credit score.

Blockchains integrate into existing systems.
Blockchain exists as a service (BaaS) or a blockchain application platform. BaaS offers groups and organizations secure connections using cloud-based services without forcing them to create and run their own blockchain, giving them more control than other existing methods. On the other hand, blockchain application platforms allow anyone without cloud services to use the technology.

Drawbacks

Blockchains incur gas fees. The most significant setback of blockchain technology is that it requires enormous amounts of energy to keep running (hence the term *gas*). Because miners must solve mathematical equations to get paid, they need mining rigs and facilities that consume a lot of electricity.

Blockchains have low scalability. As of now, blockchains can only handle a few transactions per second. When handling large volumes of transactions the system takes a long time to process, making it difficult to scale. There are, however, some solutions that have been implemented to overcome this difficulty, which we will discuss in later chapters.

Security Concerns. Since blockchains are distributed ledgers, they can be accessed by the public. Even if there are encryption layers and privacy settings, not every platform applies them (Bhagat, 2021). In short, anyone with an internet connection can monitor your transactions by viewing your wallet address, even if they cannot identify the wallet's owner. Because of this, most people resort to using third-party solutions, such as exchanges due to security concerns.

Blockchain transactions are slow. Using blockchains as a payment method can be a slow process compared to a centralized server or database since it requires miners to function. So transactions within the platform will take longer than cash or credit card transactions.

Blockchains are prone to 51% attacks. 51% attacks happen wherein one entity (e.g., a hacker) manages to control fifty percent or more of the network's hashing power, enabling them to disrupt the blockchain operations by intentionally modifying or excluding the order of transactions inside it (Binance Academy, 2022). This kind of data sabotage is possible, but there are no records of success against a Bitcoin blockchain since the network is more extensive and its security more robust.

Blockchains are inefficient. Since blockchains implement a proof of work system through mining, only one out of ten miners win (every ten minutes), while the efforts of the other nine are wasted. As more miners gradually increase their computing power by availing more advanced facilities, they also use more energy to run the mining rigs. This poses an environmental ethics issue for some.

Users are required to remember their private keys. Public keys (a lengthy string of alphanumeric characters) give ownership rights to each user on the blockchain. Each address within the blockchain also has a set of private keys. These keys open the lock to the user's safe so that they can access their funds, like a bank. Since it is difficult to remember, users may need to write it down or store its details to avoid losing access to their money forever.

The Double-Edged Sword

The blockchain network has at least two features that can be both advantageous and disadvantageous. In a way, blockchain has the potential to function as a two-edged sword.

Immutability of Information

Like most technology, Blockchain technology is not perfect. Therefore, it is not error-proof. So, the very thing that makes transactions more secure can cause problems if an error occurs. Unfortunately, an error can't be corrected since nothing can be altered (Tenorio, 2021).

Anonymity

Most users consider this feature a virtue because they trust the blockchain network and its validation of person-to-person transactions, according to Tenorio (2021). However, those who commit illegal activity can exploit the same feature because transactions aren't traceable.

Blockchain technology is promising, especially if you look at its futuristic uses. However, it is still in its infancy, requiring constant development and innovation before it can significantly benefit the public. Additionally, utilizing the technology requires facilities to handle the grunt work involved with mining, which requires lots of money and energy. No one knows for certain whether this will improve or if the technology will simply be replaced by something better.

Now that we have laid out some basics regarding the pros and cons of blockchain technology, let's move on to cryptocurrencies.

2

CRYPTOCURRENCY

WHAT IS CRYPTOCURRENCY?

C ryptocurrency serves as a digital, encrypted, and decentralized medium of exchange. Contrary to the US dollar and other fiat currencies, no central authority manages and maintains its value. Instead, the management is distributed among cryptocurrency miners across the internet. Although cryptocurrency is a novel and volatile asset class, many investors are interested. Because purchasing cryptocurrency entails risk, you need to learn about it to understand how it works.

Cryptocurrencies, similar to NFTs, are digital assets created through computer-networking software for secure trading and ownership. Individual cryptos are called tokens or coins, depending on how you use these cryptocurrencies. You may use cryptocurrencies as a unit for exchanging goods and services. Or you may keep them as stores of value. Some cryptos are used for computer networks that work on complex financial transactions.

KEY CONCEPTS OF CRYPTOCURRENCY

- **Transferability:** Conducting business with people far away from you can be seamless with crypto. Paying through crypto can be like paying cash at your local stores.
- **Privacy:** Since transactions using cryptocurrencies do not require you to provide sensitive information, there is less or no risk of

identity theft or your financial data being compromised.

- **Security:** Most cryptocurrencies like Bitcoin, Ethereum, and many others are secured with blockchain technology. They are constantly checked and verified using a considerable amount of computing power.

- **Portability:** Wherever you are, your cryptocurrency is always available to you because a financial institution or government doesn't control it. So, if anything happens to any of the global financial system's major intermediaries, your cryptocurrency is safe and secure, and you can instantly gain access to it.

- **Transparency:** Every transaction in the blockchain is open to the public. Therefore, there is no reason for anyone to manipulate the trade, adjust the rules, or change the money supply, especially on the Bitcoin and Ethereum networks.

- **Irreversibility:** Any transaction involving cryptocurrency is irreversible, unlike credit cards. This works to the advantage of merchants as it reduces the risk of fraud. Low transaction fees and eliminating intermediaries lead to enormous savings for the customers.

- **Safety:** The network on which Bitcoin operates is impossible to hack because the blockchain system that supports Bitcoin is permissionless, and the core software is open source. In short, numerous computer scientists have examined all aspects of the system, safeguarding all aspects of networks and security.

HOW DOES CRYPTOCURRENCY WORK?

You know now that a blockchain is a coded distributed ledger open to the public that records digital transactions. It is like a checkbook spread across many computers all over the world. All transactions in the blockchain are recorded in blocks and linked together in a chain.

To illustrate, imagine a journal where you record all your income and expenses daily. Each page of your journal represents each block in the blockchain. The whole journal represents the blockchain in its entirety.

With blockchain, everyone who transacts business in the blockchain has a copy of the ledger for a unified recording system. Blockchain technology logs each new transaction as they occur. Every copy of the ledger within the blockchain is updated simultaneously to ensure that all recorded information is identical and accurate. This is done via one of two mining techniques. *Mining* is bringing in new cryptocurrency in exchange for validating transactions. The two techniques used today are proof of work and proof of stake.

Proof of Work

Simon Oxenham, social media manager at Xcoins, defines proof of work as "a validation method that verifies a transaction on the blockchain using a mathematical problem, which computers have to solve" (Ashford, 2022).

Individual computers, also called miners, race to solve the puzzle that holds the key to verifying a group of transactions. The first one to solve it receives a reward equivalent to a fraction of the cryptocurrency. The race to solve the blockchain puzzles requires intense computer power and electricity.

Proof of Stake

Some use the proof of stake verification to reduce the power required in checking transactions. With this option, the number of transactions to be verified depends on the number of cryptocurrency miners willing to stake or temporarily lock up in a communal safe for the opportunity to participate. It works like collateral. Those with stakes are eligible for the verification process—your chance to be chosen or win the race is higher if you have a more significant stake. The proof of stake is more efficient than proof of work because there is no intense competition among computers.

The stake owner or the validator is chosen to validate a new group of transactions and is rewarded with cryptocurrencies. If selected, a validator's stake determines whether they can validate a new block. To discourage miners from fraud, part of their stake is forfeited if fraud is committed.

The Role of Consensus in Crypto

When verifying transactions, proof of work and proof of stake depend on consensus mechanisms. So, while each verified transaction uses individual users, each verified transaction needs to be checked and approved by the majority of ledger holders.

A hacker could not alter the blockchain record unless 51% or more of these ledgers are modified to support a fraudulent transaction. They would need an enormous number of resources to make this possible.

Can Anyone Mine Cryptocurrency?

While anyone can mine cryptocurrency, it may be more difficult in systems requiring proof of work. Let's consider the Bitcoin network. As the network grows, it becomes more complex and complicated. According to Spencer Montgomery, founder of Uinta Crypto Consulting, it also requires more power for processing (Ashford, 2022). In the past, anyone could mine using their personal computers. Today, too many people have optimized their equipment because of the competition, throwing ordinary people out of the game.

Because proof of work in cryptocurrencies requires an enormous power supply, about 0.21% of the world's electricity goes to Bitcoin mining—roughly the same amount of energy that Switzerland uses annually. However, only 60 to 80% of what a Bitcoin miner earns goes to cover the electricity cost.

While it seems too challenging for an average person to participate in a proof of work system to mine Bitcoins, the proof of stake uses less power supply. Still, it requires miners to own crypto to help validate the work. Therefore, what they own will serve as their stake, and they are chosen randomly based on the amount they stake.

WHERE DO CRYPTOCURRENCIES GET THEIR VALUE?

Supply indicates how much quantity is available to buy at a specific time, while *demand* refers to the people who desire to purchase or own the cryptocurrency. The value of the cryptocurrency is the balance of these two —supply and demand.

Also, this type of financial system is exciting and entirely new for others starting off. Therefore, value can be created from a sense of pride from being a part of a unique opportunity. Similarly, some others love paying with cryptocurrency due to the low fees compared to traditional banking systems and want other businesses to embrace this new payment method.

HOW TO USE CRYPTOCURRENCY FOR SECURE PURCHASES

Buying something securely using crypto depends on what you want. For example, suppose the merchant you want to purchase something from does not accept cryptocurrency. In that case, you may use a cryptocurrency debit card like BitPay.

If the merchant accepts cryptocurrency, on the other hand, you need to have a wallet. A cryptocurrency wallet is an application program that interacts with the blockchain, allowing users to send and receive cryptocurrency.

In transferring money from your wallet, you may manually enter the recipient's address or scan their QR code. Some service providers allow you to enter a phone number from your contacts to make it easier. Remember that your transaction processing requires validation of proof of work or proof of stake. The transaction takes ten minutes to two hours, depending on the cryptocurrency used.

HOW TO INVEST IN CRYPTOCURRENCY

You can purchase cryptocurrency on cryptocurrency exchanges like Coinbase, Bitfinex, Binance or Crypto.-com. You may also buy it from peer-to-peer networks. However, be aware that these exchanges can charge extremely high fees. Coinbase, for example, charges as much as 0.5% of your purchases plus between $0.99 to $2.99, depending on the transaction amount.

Other brokerages like Webull, Robinhood, and eToro allow you to invest in cryptocurrency by trading the popular cryptocurrencies, including Bitcoin, Dogecoin, and Ethereum. However, they also impose limitations like not allowing you to move crypto purchases outside their platform.

Previously, it wasn't easy to buy or trade cryptocurrencies. Today, even complete beginners can quickly create an account in any cryptocurrency exchange and link it to their bank accounts.

Think of it as investing in stocks. It's best not to keep all your eggs in one basket. Rather than choose only one cryptocurrency, invest in different types to spread your investment. If you want to invest in lower-risk cryptocurrencies, you might also invest in big corporations adopting blockchain technology. Among these are Bank of America, IBM, and Microsoft.

SHOULD YOU INVEST IN CRYPTOCURRENCY?

Many investors are interested in cryptocurrencies because they are easy, rewarding, and secure. As a result, a million investors hold cryptocurrencies as part of their investment portfolios. Since you can buy fractional coins, you can buy as little or as much as you want. It means you don't need to pay for the entire value of the currency. You can even buy as little as $10 worth of Bitcoin, Ethereum, or any coin you choose.

You can set up your account in any cryptocurrency exchange or have a software wallet in only a few minutes. You may use your debit or credit account when you want to buy these digital assets. Some assets like USD Coin (USDC) and Tezos offer rewards to holders just for having them. Coinbase also provides a 5% annual percentage yield (APY) when you stake Tezos on Coinbase (*What is cryptocurrency?*, n.d.).

However, because cryptocurrency is highly volatile, it is a highly speculative investment, and many financial investors don't recommend investing in them.

Let's look at the value of Bitcoin as an example. It nearly doubled in 2020 and closed at $28,000 by the end of the year. By April of the following year, it had more than doubled its value, then plummeted by July. BTC hit more than $68,900 by November 10, 2021, but dropped to $46,000 by the end of the year. At the time of writing, BTC was fluctuating around $40,000. This is only one example of crypto's volatility. It is easy to see why experts hold mixed opinions about investing in cryptocurrency.

WHY IS CRYPTOCURRENCY THE FUTURE OF FINANCE?

The use of cryptocurrency could enhance and upgrade financial services in many ways.

- Because it is digital and originated on the internet, it is the fastest, cheapest, and most straightforward way to send money, even between countries with different fiat currencies.
- Cryptocurrencies can be used when purchasing goods and services, but they also serve as

investments. With no central authority to manipulate them, crypto remains safe regardless of what happens to the government or banking industries.

- Cryptocurrencies provide equal opportunities to everyone. Anyone can access these digital currencies if they have internet access.
- Cryptocurrencies provide a comprehensive range of global opportunities for economic freedom. Their ability to cross borders facilitates free trade, especially in countries with tight government controls over the finances of their citizens.
- When there is a problem with inflation, cryptos can provide an alternative to dysfunctional fiat currencies for savings and payment.

After learning about cryptocurrencies and how they work with blockchain technology, we will briefly look at cryptocurrency mining.

3

CRYPTO MINING

You can compare digital mining to gold mining in many respects. Digital mining is a computer operation that creates new Bitcoin while tracking transactions and ownership of the cryptocurrency. Bitcoin and gold mining are both energy-intensive and have the potential to be highly financially rewarding.

A blockchain developer creates this application using several vital components and methods. In this chapter, we will use Bitcoin as an example.

WHAT IS CRYPTO MINING?

Mining, also known as crypto mining, is how you gather cryptocurrency in the blockchain. There are different types of crypto, and each requires a specific blockchain to mine that cryptocurrency. In other words, it's impossible to mine Bitcoins inside an Ethereum blockchain and vice-versa.

Crypto mining is responsible for soaring graphics card prices, computer damage worldwide, and higher power consumption. Some people think that, through this process, you can get coins after each successful mine. However, you might be fortunate to get even a fractional piece of your particular currency. After all, only one out of ten participating miners will be able to get anything after mining for ten minutes.

Cryptocurrencies are entirely digital, with no record of transactions and possession in the physical world. They are also decentralized, meaning no entities control them. This is in stark contrast to government-controlled fiat currencies. Instead, the blockchain maintains records of these transactions inside digital ledgers. These logs are distributed throughout the network for all users to see them. The large number of computers that keep track of these transactions are also called mining rigs or mining systems.

MINING COMPUTERS, RIGS, AND FARMS

In theory, anyone can create or set up a mining rig. You can obtain financing for a powerful computer with a fast graphics card, mining software, a crypto wallet for your desired cryptocurrency, and a suitable blockchain to mine.

Currently, GPU mining (crypto mining using GPUs inside graphics cards instead of CPU mining computers) is rising because it works faster. Miners like to use gaming computers with Nvidia or AMD GPUs (Nayak, 2022). And this is the reason graphics cards have become too expensive for most people to afford—supply and demand.

Using laptops for crypto mining is never encouraged because they are not equipped with suitable cooling systems to remove the heat efficiently. As a result, the more calculations the CPU or GPU does, the faster it heats up, which can cause considerable damage to your laptop over time. To avoid this, miners recommend servers and desktops customized with good heat sinks and cooling fans. Miners can also use computers with motherboards designed to link up to eight GPUs for doing rapid calculations. Some even created mining rigs to work simultaneously, giving rise to crypto mining farms.

What Is a Mining Rig?

A mining rig has all the components of a Personal Computer. You have a motherboard, RAM, CPU, GPU, power supply, and storage. In the past, miners used their personal computers with only one CPU processing power. Over time, cryptocurrency and blockchain users are becoming more innovative and developing more intricate setups with specialized equipment for maximum processing capability.

To improve efficiency, miners needed to upgrade their computers. They combined multiple high-end graphic cards to process more equations at once, requiring higher power, better cooling, and ventilation while increasing the mining costs. Again, this demand for graphics cards contributed to their scarcity and increased prices on the secondary market during the COVID-19 pandemic.

Another popular option in the mining operation of cryptocurrencies is to invest in pre-configured mining hardware like an Application-Specific Integrated Circuit (ASIC) miner (Hong, 2022). These are banks of microprocessors with built-in cooling systems. Others choose to join mining pools and combine their processing power. Whatever the team mines is divided among the members.

What Is Hash Rate?

A hash rate is how many guesses per second a rig can manage. Depending on how much processing power your mining equipment has, it can compute answers at a specific hash rate. It can be anything from mega-hashes per second (MH/s), to gigahashes per second (GH/s) or terahashes per second. (TH/s).

The mining system generates mathematical equations that miners must solve. To correctly solve the puzzle, miners must produce the correct 64-digit hexadecimal number. The first miner to get the correct number, or hash, at or below the target receives the reward assigned for that specific block. Because miners want the reward, they must have a rig capable of calculating the hash before everyone else, thus making the hash rate significant.

The difficulty in calculating each new proof of work equation does not lie in the equation. The challenge lies in how many possible answers a machine must grind through to get the correct hash. The constant calculation requires a large amount of power and energy, especially for mining farms using banks of mining rigs that run continuously.

How Do These Components Work Together in the Blockchain Ecosystem?

Let's closely examine the cryptocurrency mining process to understand how it works.

Transactions are the very foundation of cryptocurrency blockchains. You need to understand how all components come together.

To illustrate, let's say you are a crypto miner. Person B borrows 5,000 from Person A. Person B sends Person A a partial Bitcoin unit as payment. For the transaction to be deemed complete, it must be verified.

All transactions (like our example payment above) are bundled into a list and then added to a new, unconfirmed data block in the mining process. Adding this transaction to the Blockchain prevents double-spending of crypto by keeping a permanent public record. Because the record is immutable, no one can alter or manipulate it.

Once the miners add enough transactions to the block, additional information is combined with the hash from the preceding chain within the block, header data, and a new hash for the new block. (The most recent block header is combined with the nonce to generate a new hash.) Once the hash is added to the unconfirmed block, a miner node must verify it.

Let's say you are the one to solve the equation; you must shout it out to publicly inform the rest of the miners so they can verify it. The other miners in the network will verify the integrity of the unconfirmed block by reviewing it. The verification process is complicated, and the average person will not be able to decipher a hash.

Once the block is confirmed and published in the blockchain, the proof of work is complete. The coin transfer from Person B to Person A (now complete) becomes part of the blockchain once added to the block. The most recent block is then added to the end of the blockchain. This is because the blockchain ledgers are arranged chronologically.

For the ledger to stay secure from manipulation and unauthorized modification, all transactions are encrypted using public-key cryptography. They must also utilize a hash that the miner nodes on the blockchain can use to verify that each block is genuine and unaltered.

WHO UPDATES THE BLOCKCHAIN AND HOW FREQUENTLY?

Without a central regulating authority to manage and control exchanges, computers involved in the mining process are responsible for keeping the ledger and updates to the log. It is estimated that new blocks are added every ten minutes.

The blockchain is in public view, so anyone can see and update the ledger using a computer. With the proper equipment, you can generate random guesses to solve an equation the blockchain presents. If successful, you will receive a reward, and that transaction is successfully recorded. If not, you can keep guessing until you find the correct answer to the equation.

HOW DOES BITCOIN MINING WORK?

Bitcoin mining is the process that enables new Bitcoins to enter circulation. It is also a crucial component of the blockchain's ledger maintenance and is necessary for networks to confirm recent transactions. The mining process uses hardware that can solve highly complex math problems. Once a computer solves the problem, it will receive the next block of Bitcoins, and the cycle starts again.

Crypto mining is never easy since it requires facilities, time, and effort to bear fruit. Nonetheless, its appeal is comparable to the California Gold Rush of 1849, wherein prospectors flocked from all over for a chance to find (or mine) a small nugget of gold.

The Bitcoin fortunate miners receive is an incentive that persuades and inspires people to legitimize and monitor Bitcoin transactions. Because every miner shares this task, Bitcoin is said to be decentralized, so mediators are not required to monitor its operation.

REASONS WHY BITCOIN NEEDS MINERS

Blockchain mining is just a term used for the computational work done by nodes within the network to gain new coins or tokens. In comparison, miners are like auditors because of their work concerning digital ledgers. Miners prevent "double spending," which can happen in cryptocurrencies.

In a literal sense, double spending is when cryptocurrencies like Bitcoin are copied or duplicated, so two or more transactions are made using the same Bitcoin. Since cryptocurrencies are digital, there's a chance that someone will be able to do this through questionable means. Like those who check for counterfeit money, cryptocurrency miners check transactions to prevent someone from spending the same coin twice. Additionally, mining is the only way to mint or release additional cryptocurrency. Nowadays, most Bitcoins in circulation, aside from those from the Genesis Block, are minted by miners. Even if someone mines the last Bitcoin someday, the mining work will continue so that Bitcoin's network integrity will remain.

Aside from comparing digital ledgers and complex calculations, guesswork is part of what miners do on a regular basis. They do this by trying to be the first to guess the correct 64-digit hexadecimal number or hash, which is equal to or less than the blockchain's target hash. Because of statistical randomness and the need for mathematical guesswork, the possibility of guessing correctly is in the trillions. It's not something a normal human being will be able to do, no matter how hard you try. Hence, it is wise to get a computer with impressive specifications that narrow your guesswork. After all, those with powerful computers influence decisions concerning cryptocurrencies, particularly Bitcoin.

HOW TO START MINING BITCOIN

Does mining Bitcoin interest you? Anyone with computer skills can qualify for mining. It is challenging, but if you enjoy exploring emerging technologies and computers, then you might as well earn while you learn. If you're interested, here are the steps to get started in Bitcoin mining.

Choose Your Bitcoin Mining Hardware

For Bitcoin mining, you must use optimized mining hardware like a Graphics Processing Unit (GPU) or an

Application-Specific Integrated Circuit (ASIC) miner. The minimum requirements are:

- secure high-speed internet connection (at least 50 kilobytes per second)
- unrestricted data uploads and downloads (Generally, Bitcoin mining nodes use up to 200 gigabytes of data for monthly uploads and about 20 gigabytes for monthly data uploads.)

Decide Between Solo and Pooled Mining

After choosing your Bitcoin mining hardware, the next thing is to decide between mining on your own or collaborating with a team. Joining a mining pool is more predictable and consistently profitable than working solo.

Install and Configure Bitcoin Mining Software

You can now begin installing your Bitcoin mining software. There are many mining applications to choose from depending on your operating system, hardware, and other factors. Take note that you must link your mining setup to a Bitcoin wallet—one dedicated to Bitcoin. You will use this wallet to collect your rewards.

Begin Mining for Bitcoin

After fully configuring your mining rig, click the button to start the mining process. You have nothing else to do but watch your computer work for you. To be successful, mining rigs must operate for at least six hours a day. However, letting your mining rig run all the time increases your earning potential.

Monitor and Fine-Tune Your Mining Rig

Although Bitcoin mining is passive, it's not entirely a set-it-and-forget-it system. To ensure that your mining operation is working efficiently, you must monitor its performance and energy use. You never know when it will need some small configurations to improve your profitability significantly.

IF CRYPTOCURRENCY MINING IS SO SIMPLE, WHY DOESN'T EVERYONE DO IT?

Like other investing endeavors, crypto mining is not for everyone.

Crypto Mining Is Resource-Intensive

While everyone wants to take advantage of crypto mining, not everyone has the resources to do so. For one, crypto mining requires a lot of energy and better equipment to cope with the competition. Two, you must also be aware of your expenses with this process.

▷ Crypto Mining Is Expensive

Because of the high-power requirement of the mining process, you must consider the equipment costs involved. While you were once able to mine cryptocurrency using your personal computer, it's almost impossible to do so now. If your equipment has a low capacity, how can you beat others using high-tech equipment in their calculations? Therefore, having more devices and access to less expensive power is crucial if you want to get a share of the mining rewards.

▷ Hardware Damage

Choosing the wrong hardware or operating a mining configuration without proper ventilation can cause your equipment to overheat because Bitcoin mining is a highly intensive process for computers. However, if you set up your system correctly, you need not worry as there won't be any damage to your hardware beyond the normal wear and tear.

▷ Bandwidth Use

Due to the constant and regular uploading and downloading of data, Bitcoin mining requires unlimited and unmetered internet connections. If you pay for every megabyte or gigabyte used, you will encounter data caps and have your internet plan cut off because you will be using more data.

Crypto Mining and Its Environmental Effects

According to present statistics, Bitcoin mining generates up to a hundred million tons of carbon dioxide. Ethereum mining produces over fifty million tons of carbon dioxide annually. These numbers are still increasing due to higher interest in the digital trend.

This carbon dioxide pollution happens because crypto mining requires electricity for computers to work, which, in turn, consumes petroleum-based fuel. Thankfully, companies like Ethereum are exploring eco-friendly alternative technologies.

The Yield Is Not What It Used to Be

Since the supply of Bitcoin is limited to 21 million coins, mining Bitcoin is getting more complex and challenging. The number of Bitcoins created every year is cut in half. Once the target number of Bitcoin mined reaches 21 million, miners will no longer be able to mine Bitcoins, and their earnings will depend on transaction fees alone.

The reward miners receive is reducing as the number of unmined Bitcoins declines. A 50% reduction in rewards for miners happens every time another 210,000 block of Bitcoins is mined. It is estimated that this "halving" occurs every four years. When it was launched in 2009, the reward for successfully mining a Bitcoin block was 50 coins. Then in 2012, the first halving occurred and reduced the mining rewards to 25 Bitcoins. Another halving happened the same year. The most recent took place in May 2020.

Today, the current reward for mining a block of Bitcoin is 6.25 BTC, with the next halving expected to happen in 2024. Although mining becomes more difficult while rewards decrease, it will take a long time before miners can mint the entire stock of Bitcoins. Despite the challenges, miners still consider Bitcoin a lucrative endeavor since completing a single block could earn around $240,000.

Crypto Prohibition

Although crypto mining is not illegal, some places prohibit it. China, for example, has cracked down on crypto miners, sending them into hiding or forcing them to transfer to other sites. There are even countries that prohibit the use of cryptocurrencies. Crypto mining can be an exciting alternative to the traditional centralized systems currently used globally. However, it is still very taxing in terms of computational and power resources. Given that Bitcoin and Ethereum mining consume as much electricity as a small country, it makes sense why some countries across the globe prohibit this action.

Taxes

Bitcoins are taxable, like any other income-generating activity. So, monitor any profit derived from trading Bitcoins and other activities to avoid having issues with government authorities in your location.

CRYPTO MINING GAMES & SIMULATORS

Building your own mining computer can be extremely costly, so for those on a tight budget, cheaper ways exist to earn crypto while also learning about the fundamentals of mining. Here are three games that not only teach you about how mining works but also allow you to earn tokens and altcoins within the game.

Rollercoin

Rollercoin is a Bitcoin mining simulator that lets users earn Bitcoin at no starting cost. The game simulates setting up mining facilities, and challenges miners face while incentivizing users through rewards and giveaways. New users can immediately earn Satoshi (1 Satoshi = 0.00000001 Bitcoin) by playing and winning games. Players can also upgrade their mining equipment for better earning potential for other rewards such as Ethereum, Dogecoin, Binance Coin, Tether, and Solana (Granahan, 2022).

Bitcoin Miner

Bitcoin Miner is a mobile app that simulates a Bitcoin mining operation. It's a strategy and play-to-earn game that teaches players how to best optimize their small mining rig into elaborate mining farms. Although the game doesn't mine for Bitcoins, it does allow players to earn rewards such as Satoshis while using the app. You will need a Zebedee wallet to integrate with the Bitcoin Miner app.

Crypto Idle Miner

Crypto Idle Miner is a mobile simulation game where players can set up Bitcoin mining facilities, start crypto companies and reinvest earnings into the game (Granahan, 2022). It is mainly played for fun as the earning potentials are not as great as the previously mentioned games. Users can only earn the HORA token using the app, which currently cannot be withdrawn or exchanged for other currencies. In the future, this will move to the Binance Smart Chain (BSC), which is easier to exchange for other cryptocurrencies.

Crypto Miner Tycoon Simulator

Crypto Miner Tycoon Simulator is not a play-to-earn type of game, however, it does a phenomenal job of simulating the Bitcoin mining process. The game begins back in 2010 and progresses throughout the years, allowing the player to upgrade their mining operation by reinvesting their earnings. The simulator teaches how to build PCs, shows the complexities of mining facilities, and comprehensively captures the elements of owning a crypto mining business. Because there is no earning potential, nor is this game decentralized, it may not attract many interested people in NFTs. However, it does provide an educational and fun way to learn about the history and processing of mining.

In later chapters, we will discuss other play-to-earn games incorporating NFTs into the gameplay. Since you have now become well-versed in the concepts of blockchain, cryptocurrency, and crypto mining, it's time to understand how NFTs function within the blockchain.

4

NON-FUNGIBLE TOKENS (NFTS)

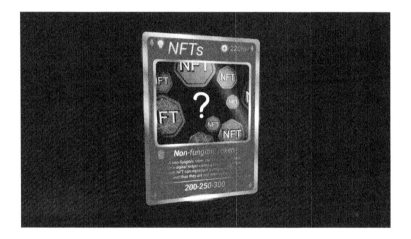

In 2021, the spotlight shone brightly on the NFT market, and people wanted to know more about this phenomenon. The NFT craze gained recognition because of the art associated with it and the use cases (or utility) tied to the token. Once you understand what makes NFTs unique and how they can be utilized, you'll understand what kind of NFT projects you'd prefer to invest in and what you will gain from doing so.

Non-fungible tokens are blockchain-based tokens minted to represent unique digital or physical assets such as artworks, collectibles, media, intellectual property, titles, gaming items, or even concert tickets. They are irreversible digital certificates of ownership and authenticity. NFTs have allowed creators to push their creative limits by employing them in clever ways. They give creators and artists a new way to display and monetize their work and grant collectors complete transparency into the chronology of ownership (provenance) and authenticity of each NFT.

Yes, you could technically screenshot an NFT and claim ownership, but you won't be able to sell the screenshot at the same price as the original. Try selling a picture you snapped of Van Gogh's *A Starry Night* at the Museum of Modern Art in New York, and you'd be hard-pressed to find a collector of that image. That's because the photo is not authentic, nor is there provenance. No one would want that photo because it can't be proven to be the original. NFTs, on the other hand, have a code that the public can trace back to its source. This code and the rights to the image are what people are purchasing.

Before the boom in the CryptoArt market, Kevin McCoy minted his NFT *Quantum* on May 2, 2014, thus becoming the first creator of and paving the way for future NFTs ("Natively Digital," n.d.). The mesmerizing heptagon-shaped pixel art with colorful pulsating lines and shapes was the first example of a piece of art that used blockchain to identify its provenance. The digital artwork was then preserved on a token on May 28, 2021, and sold for $1,472,000.

WHAT MAKES NFTS UNIQUE?

NFT ownership is managed through a unique ID and metadata to prevent duplication. Whenever someone mints an NFT, they execute the codes embedded in smart contracts that conform to their chosen token standards. The minting process creates new blocks, and once the validators check the information, it's written onto the blockchain.

Fungibility

As the name would suggest, fungibility is key to what makes an NFT unique. It simply means exchangeable or interchangeable. Take a one-dollar bill, for example. You can exchange one dollar bill for another because regardless of the serial number or date it was printed, the dollar is worth the same. The same goes for cryptocurrencies. You can exchange one Bitcoin for another Bitcoin because they are fungible.

On the other side of the coin is the concept of non-fungibility. You can't interchange non-fungible items with each other. Each NFT token has rare properties with different values. One token cannot be exchanged for another because each is valued individually.

Let's take a trip to Paris, for example. Before going through security, you must have a boarding pass (a ticket to ride). This has your name, departure and arrival information, boarding time, and seat number. It is different from someone else's airplane ticket. Each passenger's ticket is unique and cannot be exchanged for another's. They are non-fungible.

To explore how NFTs are unique from each other and, therefore, non-fungible, let us use the digital collection known as Sloties. This is a collection of 10,000 unique slot machine looking NFTs created on the Ethereum blockchain that have multiple use benefits to those who own them. Each Slotie has its own unique characteristics with its own degree of rarity. These traits include different designs for the eyes, ears, mouth, skin, hat, clothes, and background, as well as features for utility, including rake back, breeding availability, and rewards or shares for holding the NFT.

Slotie NFTs. Notice the difference in attributes, thus making both unique and one-of-a-kind.

Proof of Ownership

One advantage of NFTs is that they are all unique and linked to one address. They can be bought and sold on any market associated with the blockchain where it was minted. All you'll need is your wallet's public address to do so. The "token" of an NFT is the proof of originality, and your private key serves as proof of ownership. The public key belonging to the content creator acts as proof of authenticity because it is a part of its transaction history and can distinguish the original from a counterfeit.

Scarcity

NFTs are popular because their creators decide the supply, which affects their overall value. Concert organizers limit how many attendees enter their venue by restricting the number of tickets; in the same way, NFT creators can use scarcity to drive up the value of their creations. An ideal approach is to circulate several NFTs in the market for the first few weeks to get attention and then control the number in circulation as demand increases.

Royalties

Some NFTs pay royalties to their creators, which is a huge benefit, especially for musicians who turn their songs into NFTs and sell them on the market. Royalty percentages can be set, in most cases, at a minimum of ten percent. Platforms like Zora.co and Foundation.app apply this system to encourage artists and boost their earnings.

The Difference Between NFTs and Cryptocurrency

Cryptocurrency is just that, currency. Therefore, it is fungible and has economic value. Although they are both built using blockchain technology, crypto is used to purchase the majority of NFTs on the market today.

WHY DO PEOPLE BUY NFTS?

People have different reasons for buying NFTs nowadays, aside from making money. Some invest in them because they like that they are volatile assets, while others buy NFTs because they used to collect memorabilia or toys as a kid. Whatever your reasons for wanting to dive into the NFT space, it is undeniable that they have been rising in popularity and value in recent years. In 2021 alone, there were plenty whose values skyrocketed. (CryptoPunks and Bored Ape Yacht Club NFTs are only two examples.)

Aesthetics

Some people see the aesthetic value of NFTs, especially those that display digital art. For them, investing is very profitable now that the world is steadily moving toward a digital future where people spend most of their time online. Having a collection of NFTs right now would be very profitable in many ways sometime in the future.

Status

Some see NFTs as a status symbol. For example, the artist Mike Winkelmann, also known as Beeple, sold his collage of 5,000 images called *Everydays* as an NFT for $69.3 million at Christie's auction house ("NFTs and Crypto," 2021). Beeple had pledged to create one piece of art every day starting in 2007, and this NFT was the result. After Twobadour purchased this top-of-the-line and highly respected work of art from Beeple, people began buying other NFTs from the artist. They sought to obtain social status from owning a piece of digital art connected to the artist.

Fun Investing

The highly regarded qualities of the blockchain lured small-time investors into joining the cryptocurrency bandwagon. These investors now have their eyes on NFTs, and many are buying digital art from their favorite artists. The allure of collecting NFTs like you would memorabilia, toys, action figures, trading cards, and art has drawn many to the market.

WHY DO SOME AVOID NFTS?

Some avoid NFTs because the idea that they will make money with something utterly unfamiliar to them is difficult to envision. They are unsure whether cryptocurrencies or NFTs have any actual long-term investment value. People also doubt the security of the NFTs they buy because many websites are untrustworthy or have phony URLs. In addition, the NFT purchasing and selling procedure and the components that go along with it are foreign to many people. They are also worried about the legal ramifications of NFTs.

ACCORDING TO THE EXPERTS

Let's look at two contrasting views regarding NFTs. Are they a fad, or are they the future?

Andrew Shirley

Here are some points by Andrew Shirley, editor of *The Wealth Report* at Knight Frank, on why he believes NFT won't last long (Harley & Shirley, 2021):

- NFTs exist only because of the pandemic. NFTs will survive as long as the Covid-19 pandemic lasts. Andrew Shirley believes that NFTs' staying power will fade once the first surge of excitement around it disappears.
- Demand for NFTs will soon start to wane. The originality and uniqueness of the artwork don't make them valuable. Collectible items have these traits, but there's no demand for them.
- There is an oversupply of NFTs. Although NFTs are verifiable through the blockchain, they may soon lose their allure when more people flock to this space and flood the market with video clips, images, and other art pieces. When there's too much supply, the demand will surely decrease, and soon enough, people will lose interest in NFTs.

- Millennials are the significant users of NFTs. Although millennials with deep pockets made up the biggest part of the market in 2021, this tech-savvy generation does have environmental concerns. Since NFTs and cryptocurrency consume a lot of power, many are apprehensive about buying and selling using blockchain technology.
- There are security risks. Crypto hacks that thrive on the internet could make some people reluctant to indulge in the digital craze, making it impossible for NFTs to succeed in the long run.
- There is cynicism behind NFTs. Money seems to be the motivating factor for buying NFTs, as you hear about people selling their NFTs for hundreds of thousands of dollars. Art should cater to people's emotions and creativity, not financial gain alone. And since CryptoArt isn't tangible, nor can it be displayed on the wall, it will soon lose its appeal for many art enthusiasts.

Flora Harley

On the other hand, Flora Harley, the deputy editor of *The Wealth Report* at Knight Frank, believes otherwise.

These are Flora's opinions in defense of NFTs (Harley & Shirley, 2021):

- NFTs are unique, and their ownership is provable. Beeple's art, among other digital art, can be downloaded, printed, and hung on a wall. With NFTs, you have a way to prove that you own that piece of art and that it is, in fact, authentic and original. This is not like a bank where you keep your valuables in a vault. With NFTs, you don't need a third party to safeguard your assets.

- NFTs are not just digital art. Almost everything, digital or real-world, can be sold as an NFT. This can include concert tickets, audio clips, or a video of celebrities' famous moments, such as LeBron James's famous dunk on NBA's Topshot. You may also hold ownership of real estate and other tangible properties. The adoption and offerings of NFTs are still in their infancy, and there will be further uses for NFTs in the future.

- NFT artists and creators have more control over their creations and can profit from them. The transaction is made directly between the seller and the buyer. At the same time, a part of the proceeds can go straight to the artist or musician or donated to non-profitable organizations. Anyone can resell intangible assets like music albums and paintings. However, the original artists do not receive any royalties from the resale. With NFTs, the designated benefactor can receive royalties on future sales depending on their design and how well the contract is structured. But that's not always the case. You can resell NFTs without the original designer or creator receiving any royalties.

- The value lies in the eyes of the beholder. Some people have doubts about the value of NFTs when anyone can create them. The first tweet ever was turned into an NFT by one of Twitter's founders and sold for $2.9 million. But an NFT of that caliber only had value because it was created by Jack Dorsey and not by Joe Anybody. Anyone can make an NFT of something, but that NFT is only worth as much as someone is willing to pay for it at any given moment. With celebrities and influencers causing the NFT bubble to inflate, more hype is being generated, creating more interest, and leading to more informed decision-making when investing in this space. When many people understand NFTs and their uses, more may adopt and discover the value in these digital assets.

THE POSSIBILITIES OF NFTS

People have different views when it comes to NFTs. While some analysts see NFTs as limited to digital arts and limited-edition topics, others see NFTs' immense potential in terms of work, social value, and economy. One NFT expert, Andrew Steinwold, claimed that while crypto alters value, finance, governance, organization, money, the internet, etc., NFTs will change human society and culture (Steinwold, 2020).

You can use NFTs in digital content, gaming items (i.e., in-game equipment or characters), collateral, investments, domain names, and physical objects. Nowadays, NFTs artists turn their digital artwork into NFTs without significant benefits or use-cases for the holder. But creators are discovering utility to embed within them as more and more people begin to see the advantage of tying real-world items to NFTs.

Building Community

NFTs allow artists to directly sell their artworks to their fans, supporters, and followers, thus removing the intermediaries from the transaction. They pave the way for the comeback of the conventional art community where fans directly support their favorite artists. With NFTs, a follower could help a rising artist by buying their art pieces and profit from them later when their value increases. They can also help to promote them.

Today, artists and creators can socially engage and directly transact with their fans and followers. According to Buchanan Kesonpat, a blockchain entrepreneur, the community can benefit through redeemable real-world rewards and tokens. The community is free to voice its opinions and be heard (Kesonpat, 2020).

The far-reaching, future possibilities for NFT online communities are even more interesting. Currently, social media platforms are centralized in that the power is concentrated among a small group of people who dictate who gets to stay and who gets to leave their platform. However, in the NFT space, credible experts suggest that NFTs could be the beginning of virtual states, where the holders have voting power and can govern themselves (Authors, 2021). This act of self-governance is also known as a Decentralized Autonomous Organization (DAO).

Gaming Potential

Game developers are currently using NFTs to boost in-game economies, which benefits players within the gaming industry in a huge way. One of these benefits is that you can change the ownership of the digital asset. Take the video game League of Legends, a multiplayer online battle arena (MOBA) genre developed by Riot Games, as an example. Let's say you buy a skin for one of your favorite champions. Unfortunately, you just spent your hard-earned money to buy an in-game item that could potentially disappear if the game developers decide to pull the plug on the game. That's because that item is technically never yours, to begin with. It belonged to Riot Games, the game developer. Now with NFTs, you own the object or character you purchase and can sell it to someone else.

Because NFTs record ownership of unique in-game items, you can sell them to other players once you're done with the game or want to buy a different item within the game. As issuers of the NFT, the game developers earn royalties each time a player sells it to another player on the secondary marketplace. This benefits both the consumer and the business and encourages more buying and selling of game items. And since the blockchain has a record, in-game NFTs will outlive the game itself, becoming digital memorabilia with value outside the game.

For example, The Kingdom Warrior NFT project is a collection of character-based NFTs aimed at unifying the story of these characters into music, books, video games, and other creative mediums.

A Kingdom Warrior (#1950) NFT I won during a five-day Challenge.

Owning one of the Kingdom Warrior NFTs bestows several utility benefits ("Kingdom Warriors," n.d.). These include:

- auto staking with the future on-chain token
- multiplied play-to-earn (P2E) earnings potential
- one community DAO vote per NFT
- an annual pass to a VIP event

- a free e-book of the novel
- becoming part of a future drop whitelist
- ability to make affiliate commissions through NFT sales

Owning three of these NFTs also allows the holder to obtain future airdrops of concept art NFTs, a signed copy of the novel, and early access to everything related to Kingdom Warriors. And lastly, owning ten or more Kingdom Warrior NFTs includes all the previously mentioned benefits, plus a custom 1-of-1 NFT and a seat on the board of directors.

Not only are these use-cases available to the holder, but for each NFT sold, a part of the sales is donated to the Precious Kids Foundation in Uganda, Africa. NFTs can be used to benefit the owner, creator, and the world around us. You just need to know which projects are worth investing in.

NFTs and DeFi

Decentralized Finance (DeFi) is a term used collectively for financial services or products that run on the blockchain. They differ from traditional financial services because there is no centralized authority, and the markets are always open.

The NFT and DeFi space are finding ways to work together and offer financial services to people who post their NFTs as collateral to borrow stablecoins. This potential only exists because of the infrastructure on which DeFi and NFTs operate. One day, you could even use an NFT of your house or car as collateral to secure a decentralized loan.

NFTs as an Investment

CryptoArt investors say that the impact of a pandemic, the surging price of Bitcoin, and the increasing distrust in US dollars created a perfect storm. In the past year, crypto creators and artists have drawn more attention to the NFT marketplaces with flashy sales. Beeple, became famous in the history of NFT when he sold crypto artwork for nearly $70 million (Chan & O'brien, 2021). Other artists like Grimes likewise made millions just a few hours after listing their crypto art pieces (Kastrenakes, 2021a).

THE VALUE OF NFTS

If you question the value of NFTs and wonder why they are such a big deal, then let's see why Gary Vaynerchuk believes they are valuable (Garyvee, 2021).

Ten years ago, Gary Vaynerchuk predicted the coming of virtual currency as the next big wave. And all this came from watching people interact with Farmville. Farmville was a popular and simple game on Facebook where people could plant, grow, and harvest virtual crops. Observing how people spent real money buying virtual sheep, he had a moment of inspiration. Gary realized that people were becoming more interested in going digital and displaying this through their purchasing behavior.

NFTs that represent pieces of inventory people own in digital form would be the new conversation piece in the real world. In the same way we communicate by wearing popular clothing brands or logos, NFTs are used to convey a message we are trying to portray in the digital realm. For Gary, they reflect human behavior on a larger scale.

They will integrate into the world's history, like the internet in the 90s and social media in the early 2000s. They will fuse many of his collecting, flipping, creative, business, and community-building interests. Even then, observations told him that many NFTs enthusiasts like him were watching, listening, and learning, including people like Scott Belsky and Kevin Rose. So, Gary now encourages people to learn and understand how significant this shift will be in the future.

WHAT ABOUT PHYSICAL ITEMS?

Although creating an NFT of physical items isn't as nuanced as minting a digital item, many projects still tokenize real estate, sneakers, and physical trading cards. Since NFTs act as deeds, you can buy a 1986 Fleer Michael Jordan rookie trading card using crypto and receive an NFT stating that you own the physical card so long as you hold the NFT. The moment you sell the NFT, you essentially forfeit or transfer ownership to the buyer. A company called Blokpax is an excellent example of this, giving the owners of the NFT the option to trade in the NFT for the physical card. This digital deed could be a precedent for buying a car or home, allowing the NFT to serve as the title to either of those physical assets.

SMART CONTRACTS

Smart contracts are necessary for the functioning of NFTs. These contracts are sales agreements between the seller and buyer of the NFT. These fragments of software code allow the entire network to store information on the NFT itself. Smart contracts govern various actions, such as transferring NFTs and verifying ownership during transaction initiation. In addition, a smart contract allows the network to store the information when the NFT transaction is complete, making it accessible when necessary. It also ensures that the stored information is immutable and transparent. In addition, smart contracts make it possible for someone to have permanent identification information and make NFTs unique and irreplicable. This scarcity is why NFTs have value.

What Does the Smart Contract Cover?

Smart Contracts cover the rights sold. What rights, you may ask? That depends. In most cases, the Copyrights will remain with the work's creator, while only ownership rights transfer during the sale. Buying an NFT doesn't necessarily mean that all rights are transferred to you unless the contract explicitly says otherwise. Take the Kingdom Warrior NFT I won in a 5-day challenge, for example. The license is a shared license that allows me to use it commercially within this book but does not allow me to create a separate NFT using the same image. Once I sell the NFT, I am no longer the owner, and all rights will transfer to the new owner.

How Do Smart Contracts Verify Authenticity?

Smart Contracts authenticate ownership of NFTs. The data embedded into the NFT can trace the history of the token regarding its development and availability on the blockchain. Verification of all the metadata linked to the NFT and its associated wallet address is on the blockchain. This information is open to the public. Because of an NFT's anonymous nature, you cannot trace it back to a person or specific work in the real world. However, most platforms will require the creator or user to verify their identity manually before buying, selling, or creating NFTs.

Standards of Smart Contracts for NFTs

Like with physical coins, NFTs are minted. The smart contract code verifies the qualities of the NFT and adds them to the appropriate blockchain (AlexWGomezz, n.d.). Smart contracts have many established token standards. However, Ethereum is the most frequently used and preferred by companies due to its scalability and digital influence.

▷ **ERC-721 Token Standard**

The ERC-721 standard describes how to build NFTs on the Ethereum blockchain. This standard defines the ins and outs of the smart contract and requires two bits of information: the **Token's ID** and the **Smart Contract Address**. Unlike most other tokens, it is an open standard, which makes it unique.

▷ ERC-1155 Token Standard

The ERC-1155 is a token standard used for NFTs. It is a multi-token standard that allows its smart contract to represent multiple tokens simultaneously. This standard draws from the ERC-20 and ERC-721 standards, while improving the efficiency of transferring more significant numbers of tokens without having to approve each token contract individually.

Now that you know some of the basics, let's take a look at one of the largest platforms used in conjunction with NFTs.

5

THE ETHEREUM VIRTUAL MACHINE

Are you aware of the existence of Ether (ETH)? In the world of cryptocurrency, Ether is the second-largest crypto in terms of market cap next to Bitcoin. However, it is important to distinguish Ether, the crypto or digital asset, from Ethereum, the network.

Ethereum works with both digital assets and blockchain technology. However, it uses the smart contract feature of blockchain at its core. Today, with Ethereum Virtual Machine (EVM), developers can create programs using smart contracts for different purposes.

From niche technology, blockchain has broken into the mainstream because blockchain can be applied to many sectors and is not just limited to finance and technology. With its global impact, it has the potential to transform many different industries. Understanding Ethereum and Ethereum Virtual Machine is an excellent place to start if you are interested in anything blockchain, crypto, or anything NFT-related. To better understand Ethereum Virtual Machine, let's first define it.

DEFINING ETHEREUM VIRTUAL MACHINE

The Ethereum Virtual Machine (EVM) is a platform for developers to create decentralized applications (dApps) on the Ethereum network (Nibley, 2021b). It is where all Ethereum accounts and smart contracts are stored and serves as the bedrock of the network's entire operating structure. In addition, it is the EVM's role to deploy several extra functionalities to the blockchain, ensuring that users face fewer issues on the distributed ledger.

THE PURPOSE OF THE ETHEREUM VIRTUAL MACHINE

The EVM is responsible for determining the overall state of Ethereum in each block of the blockchain. Like other blockchain-based networks, Ethereum also has its native cryptocurrency, the Ether (ETH), which maintains a database of transactions through a distributed ledger. Ethereum enforces specific rules on how users can use the network and has an additional layer of functionality because of its smart contract feature. This second layer of security is known as the "distributed state machine."

We know Ethereum's state is an extensive database that holds all ETH accounts and balances. But are you aware it is also a machine state capable of changing with each new block following a set of predetermined rules that can execute any kind of machine code? The Ethereum Virtual Machine's role is to define the specific rules that determine how the machine changes its state during each new block.

BENEFITS OF ETHEREUM VIRTUAL MACHINE

Anyone Can Create Their Own DApp

The development of the Ethereum Virtual Machine allows anyone to create their own dAapp. As a result, this software provides unending potential in terms of its use. Moreover, the technology isn't limited to any group in particular—financial or otherwise.

Unlimited Potential

The recent association of EVM with NFTs proves the endless possible uses of EVM. For example, with the advent of NFTs, anyone can now create digital items and sell them in digital marketplaces, which wasn't possible before.

DOWNSIDES OF THE ETHEREUM VIRTUAL MACHINE

Despite the upsides of the Ethereum Virtual Machine, it also has its downsides. Here are some that users identified:

Not Quite Decentralized

Amazon Web Service hosts most of the nodes within the Ethereum network. Suppose the company chooses to stop hosting Ethereum, thereby shutting down the server and the nodes contained within the Ethereum Network. In that case, the possibility exists that this could damage and destroy the operation of the whole network.

Technical Knowledge Is Needed

EVM requires technical skills like coding. So, you can't do much if you aren't literate in the computer language. However, more user-friendly interfaces exist, and NFTs are a good example. Graphical User Interface (GUIs) developed by designers on sites like Dribble.com, Fiverr, and Upwork allow users to create NFTs and use marketplaces where minting occurs.

Network Congestion Causes High Gas Fees

When there is network congestion, users must expect high gas fees, which is the number one downside for NFTs users. While this will not impact users sending large transactions, it could impact users sending smaller transactions. It likewise creates issues for decentralized applications when several users use them simultaneously. Creating many transactions and interacting with the dApp smart contracts can slow down or cease the process when gas fees soar.

WHAT IS TURING-COMPLETENESS?

When trying to get familiar with EVM, you will encounter the term *Turing-completeness.* Alan Turing, a renowned scientist who developed ideas around what a hypothetical computer or thinking machine can do, inspired the term *Turing-complete* (EVM Explained, 2021). When they say the EVM is Turing-complete, it means that the machine goes by a set of data processing rules in solving problems and not through thought-processing as humans do. Other designers have subsequently derived a virtual version using the same operating principles from Turing's physical idea of machine processing.

A Turing machine embodies Turing's concept of non-human (machine) thinking. The thinking process of the device operates through algorithms. For example, a machine can process a line of symbols or functions in a tape reel that can move backward and forward. It also can change. However, it can only focus on one state at a time. If you understand the focus of statefulness, you will find it easy to grasp how EVM works.

That reel of tape corresponding to the computer's memory is limitless and is only bound by physical limitations. Therefore, when the computer is required to follow instructions, only physical constraints can limit the data applied to such instructions. By adding to the length of the tape reel, you can add more memory. As this comprises the basic principles of its concepts and architecture, it is fundamental to understanding the Ethereum Virtual Machine.

ETHEREUM VIRTUAL MACHINE FEATURES

A Distributed State Machine

Since you are now familiar with the concept of Bitcoin after having discussed it in the previous chapters, you will realize that it is straightforward. It deals with transactions on the virtual machine and is limited to a decentralized distributed ledger.

The Ethereum network is much more extensive in scope. It is not limited to a distributed ledger but is an upgrade from its predecessor. The Ethereum network describes it as a distributed state machine that allows Ethereum to hold the entire machine state, including all data and accounts. The distributed machine state changes with every block according to specific fixed rules determined by the EVM.

The Ethereum protocol utilizes smart contracts. These are coded instructions interacting with the EVM, covering many aspects of a human agreement or simulating them. This is why Ethereum is much more complex than Bitcoin.

While Ethereum has a complex structure, its developer-facing programming language is simple, easy to learn, and user-friendly, attracting more ecosystem contributors. By design, the language that dApps and smart contracts use is relatively simple and mimics human communication patterns. It attempts to be more user-friendly in its syntax. The machine uses the same syntax to perform its functions.

Smart Contracts on the EVM

To fully understand Ethereum Virtual Machine, you must first understand what a smart contract is. A smart contract between two parties is an agreement written in codes. It is self-executing and needs no central authority, enforcement system, or regulatory framework. Therefore, anonymous parties are allowed to transact business all over the world. The implementation of smart contracts does not depend on any legal system or enforcement mechanism. Rather, it is made possible because of the design of the Ethereum network.

An American computer scientist, Nick Szabo, who first proposed it in 1994, defined *smart contracts* as, "computerized transaction protocols executed based on agreement" (Smart Contracts Explained, 2021). Having created Bit Gold in 1998, Szabo made a virtual currency long before the creation of Bitcoin. He designed the smart contract to extend the functionality of transferring value electronically. Szabo likewise proposed using smart contracts to include synthetic assets like bonds and derivatives and to create securities formed through the combinations of different financial instruments.

Smart contracts are immutable and do not compromise when they operate through multiple notes (EVM

Explained, 2021). Hence, the EVM consists of the following features:

▷ Deterministic

Determinism is crucial to the foundations of the Ethereum Virtual Machine. A program is deterministic when it provides the same results to the same data inputs regardless of numerous code executions. It is essential because dApps on Ethereum can handle large financial transactions at any given time. Therefore, knowing how the code will respond at every execution stage is critical.

▷ Isolated

Another significant trait of smart contracts is that they operate in an isolated environment facilitated by virtual machines and Docker containers. Docker containers aren't deterministic by design. The creation of virtual machines enabled this feature.

For the system to contain bugs and hacks, isolation is mandatory within a smart contract. This feature safe-guards the underlying protocol if issues arise.

▷ Terminable

Because EVM is Turing-complete, its smart contract can hypothetically solve any problem. However, there is no assurance that smart contracts can complete all operations within a given time frame. Therefore, it is critical to include a terminating mechanism, creating precise limits to resolve issues.

For example, as part of the incentive mechanism of the network, developers introduced the concept of gas to facilitate traffic, whereby gas fees will determine which functions take priority. The machine will automatically stop operations once gas limits deplete.

THE EVM ECONOMY

The Ethereum Virtual Machine creates an economy. Through gas rewards, it fosters a peer-to-peer Turing-Completeness, using existing resources to run programs. The EVM is essential to the protocol as it opens its network to anyone who wants to join and execute its code. The outcome of any executive is guaranteed through fully deterministic smart contracts, as previously discussed.

Before executing any smart contract, the protocol measures the gas cost to protect the rewards (gas incentives) and priority system. To ensure all transactions conducted within the blockchain are valid, Ethereum employs validators. The sender's funds are enough to pay for the smart contract execution and assure users that the EVM won't run into exceptions during the implementation process.

HOW DOES THE ETHEREUM VIRTUAL MACHINE WORK?

The Ethereum Virtual Machine is like other virtual machines that perform computations. It is a part of the Ethereum network responsible for executing and deploying the smart contract. While it does not engage in simple value transfers, it computes updates to the network's state.

The EVM is a computer system that manages millions of smart contracts and transactions across the globe. It has permanent data storage, decentralized nodes, and stack-based architecture, which stores all in-memory values on a stack. EVM uses native hashing and word size of 256 bits to enable elliptic curve operations (Tang, 2021).

The EVM consists of many addressable data components, such as the ROM, an immutable program code native to hashing which contains the executed smart contract bytecode, and a volatile memory with each location initialized to zero. The execution order is organized outside the EVM since clients of Ethereum comb through verified blocks to see which smart contract to deploy. The EVM has no scheduling capacity, and the Ethereum is like a single-threaded world computer without a system interface or hardware support.

The EVM's instruction set is Turing-complete. It allows contract deployment on the network to do anything that other regular computers can do. Popular tasks include creating fungible tokens that comply with the ERC-20 standard. It likewise allows the creation of NFTs under the ERC-721 standards. Decentralized finance markets, crowdfunding, and games use these tokens with different properties.

However, some programs take time to execute, which creates a halting problem, putting Ethereum at risk of running a never-ending program. The problem is that you can't just label it as an infinite loop by checking its code. Execution must occur. So, without a scheduling system, it will stall the operation of the network. Thankfully, Ethereum was able to deal with the issue cleverly.

WHAT IS ETHEREUM GAS?

To resolve the schedule issue, Ethereum uses a concept known as "gas." In the EVM environment, gas is the precious resource that allows code execution. Every code carries a gas fee. Before computation, one must specify a gas limit. The EVM ceases to operate as soon as the transaction gas fuel depletes. The EVM can run any program using a certain amount of computation power. Therefore, it is only a pseudo-Turing complete machine.

Any network participant can pay to increase the gas block limit—the maximum value of the gas for the transaction—since these limits are not frozen or resolute. Over time, the network may be able to increase this upper limit. Yet, at this stage, the number of computational steps is limited by the gas available for any smart contract execution. Transactions beyond the gas block limit automatically terminate. Since its inception, the EVM hasn't changed much and has had several transactions co-occurring. This traffic jam can create a bottleneck and affect how efficiently the blockchain operates on the Ethereum network.

THE SIGNIFICANCE OF THE ETHEREUM VIRTUAL MACHINE

The EVM is critical to the Ethereum platform and crucial to its consensus engine. With its trustless, deterministic environment accessible to anyone who wants to execute a code, Ethereum is leading a change in how the world approaches finance and money.

For every instruction on the EVM, the network monitors the cost of the transaction in gas units. It ensures that the blockchain doesn't run infinite loops. It guarantees that validators or miners will receive at least the gas fees, even if the transaction fails, preventing any contract from running longer than the system allows.

Validators assure the EVM that once Ethereum receives a transaction, it doesn't run into any exceptions during the deployment and verifies the transaction. Instead of charging per transaction like Bitcoin, participants get assigned only per software instruction. Because of the Turing-complete environment, Ethereum can be considered a globally decentralized computer for general purposes and could impact the future as the internet does today.

ETHEREUM 2.0—THE FUTURE OF THE EVM

The EVM still has flaws. Although the EVM is internally consistent, it wasn't built with real-world execution. Ethereum developer Lane Rettig states that during its creation, design thinking needed to be implemented but wasn't. Many prominent Ethereum development community members also share the sentiment of Rettig's comment (Dugan, 2020).

However, when it shifted to eWASM on Ethereum 2.0, the network showed that it was starting to prioritize efficiency over correctness. They designed the WebAssembly to be closer to the actual hardware instructions, resulting in much better translating code logic. Because WASM maps one-to-one with machine instructions, this enables significant network performance changes.

All the NFTs and other dApps on Ethereum are under the Ethereum Mainnet blockchain. According to Ethereum, they will soon merge with the Beacon Chain, which introduced the proof-of-stake system (Upgrading Ethereum, n.d.). This merge is set to take place toward the end of 2022. Ethereum 2.0 will shift away from the proof-of-work mining validation process and fully transition into a less energy-intensive and more efficient system overall. The shift will eventually allow Ethereum to scale more and store more data with the introduction of Sharding in the following years. Ethereum expects to reduce the blockchain technology's energy consumption by 99.95% with this change. Overall, it means cheaper gas fees, more security within the network, and happier, more eco-conscious investors.

The future for Ethereum looks bright as the Internet is the most valuable global network we have today. What Ethereum and blockchain technology could someday attain is something everyone can look forward to. These technologies have paved the way for the creation, distribution, and circulation of NFTs worldwide.

Now that you have a better understanding of how NFTs work on the blockchain, the following chapters will help you decide whether this is the investment you want to pursue.

6

NFT MARKETPLACES

Currently, the NFT hype is in full swing integrating into social media platforms such as TikTok and companies like Nike. Even the top celebrities worldwide are now interested in NFTs, making it the latest trend.

In this time of the NFT gold rush, many companies are now using the blockchain and minting non-fungible tokens. As a result, NFT marketplaces currently exist to display, buy, and sell NFTs, allowing creatives and the public to trade, mint, auction, and even collect them.

CHOOSING AN NFT MARKETPLACE

Keep in mind that not all existing marketplaces use the same system. For example, some marketplaces leverage the Ethereum Network using innovative technologies; others support liquidity mining, and others offer improved security and lower gas fees. Some even implement custom features for community governance that give miners voting power to decide policies and procedures. Before choosing your preferred market-place, you must consider certain factors that affect how the NFT can transfer hands.

The Token Standard

Different NFT Marketplaces might serve the same function but are not precisely the same. Some plat-forms use many versions of token standards (see Chapter 4). In contrast, others prefer using native ones based on their blockchain. As of now, here are some of the token standards that are in use:

- ERC-721 focuses on displaying rare collectibles mainly on the Ethereum network as it is the first standard used for NFTs.
- ERC 998 is used for trading various tokens on a single ownership transfer for long-term gains.
- ERC 1155 is used for leveraging the same smart contracts to hold both fungible and non-fungible tokens as well as in-game items and currencies.

- FA2 token is used for its unified token interface that supports fungible, non-fungible, transferable, non-transferable, and multi-asset contracts.
- The Flow-NFT standard is written in Cadence (its language) and allows developers to upgrade or update the smart contracts incrementally.

Price Discovery

Even though it is a newer feature, price discovery is essential for buyers and sellers alike. If you're using mintable artwork, this feature allows you to determine and estimate the right price to attract potential buyers. At the same time, the buyers can use this feature to carefully make buying decisions and avoid spending a fortune on worthless collectibles.

Wallet Compatibility

Without a compatible digital wallet, you cannot buy or sell NFTs and move funds from your bank account or credit card. Be sure to choose a marketplace that supports various digital wallets (more on this in Chapter 8). Furthermore, the integration should be seamless and easy, provide a good marketing experience, and keep your funds secure.

Token Fractionalization

An NFT can be expensive, especially if it's a land title or a digital artwork. Selling it may seem impossible and could take some time. However, using token fractionalization, the creator or seller of the NFT can assign ownership in bits via a smart contract instead of waiting for a buyer or the highest bidder if sold at auction. At the same time, the buyers can also become part owners of the NFT without having to spend a massive fortune on it.

Incentives

Whether we like it or not, offering discounts, referral bonuses, or profit-sharing is part of doing business in the NFT world; this is a gesture of goodwill toward loyal customers. It may become difficult to deal with those marketplaces that do not offer incentives early on, so consider that before diving into a particular platform.

Verification Process

Any company dealing with money should have a secure verification process, and the same system applies to NFT marketplaces. In other words, the less secure the platform is, the more likely you will lose your hard-earned money. The verification process might include two-factor authentication such as code or biometrics, captcha, and security challenges. It may also implement a "know your customer" (KYC) verification service.

POPULAR NFT MARKETPLACES

OpenSea (Website: Opensea.io)

As the leader in NFT sales, OpenSea supports multiple digital assets on its platform. Because of that, it is the largest marketplace out there today. OpenSea has been praised for growing rapidly, with a net worth of 13 billion dollars (Charles X, 2021. It is free to sign up and browse the plethora of offerings. Their marketplace currently supports more than 150 different tokens, making it a great place to start when dealing with NFTs. Collectors can find the following categories of NFTs on OpenSea:

- art
- collectibles
- domain names
- music
- photography
- sports
- trading Cards
- utility
- virtual worlds

OpenSea is user-friendly, which makes NFTs easy to create, sell, and buy. Minting is also free—great news for creators. They have a few options for auctioning NFTs, or you can choose to set a fixed price for them. They only charge a fee of 2.5% for sales and a one-time gas fee for listing your NFTs. The downside is that since OpenSea operates on the Ethereum blockchain, the gas prices for transactions are very high.

Axie Marketplace (Website: marketplace. axieinfinity.com)

Axie Marketplace, the online shop for the play-to-earn (P2E) game Axie Infinity, is where you can purchase all your needed in-game items and characters. Axies are fictitious creatures that can be bought and sold on the Axie Marketplace. In this NFT game, you can use your

Axies to fight against others. Axie Shards, or Axie Infinity tokens, were built using the Ethereum network. They can be purchased or sold on other NFT marketplaces and cryptocurrency exchanges like Coinbase.

Rarible (Website: rarible.com)

Rarible is high among the top-rated NFT marketplaces. Like OpenSea, Rarible offers NFTs of videos, art, collectibles, and music that have been created, sold, and bought on the platform. They are a multichain marketplace and support Ethereum, Flow, and Tezos. Polygon is also in its beta stage on Rarible. You can choose your audience, carbon footprint, and how much you are willing to pay for fees. Rarible takes a 2.5% commission from both the seller and the buyer. Minting is free, depending on which blockchain you select, and you have the option to set a royalty rate ranging from 5 to 10%. The platform also uses a Rarible crypto token called RARI awarded to engage users who vote on future changes. Rarible allows fixed-priced listings to purchase with a credit card, but you can only pay for auctions with cryptocurrency.

SuperRare (Website: superrare.com)

A marketplace designed for digital creators, SuperRare offers a variety of digital art, videos, and images. These single-edition NFTs can be bought and sold using ETH and are not available on any other marketplace. Super-Rare is described as a cross between Christie's auction house and Instagram and has a solid community. All their artists are hand-selected and attract serious digital art collectors. It has an elegant layout, which makes it intuitive and user-friendly. However, you need approval to sell NFTs, they take 15% of the first sale, and gas prices are high for each transaction since it uses the Ethereum blockchain. As an artist, you'll get 10% royalty each time your art sells (after the initial sale).

NBA Top Shot Marketplace (Website: nbatopshot.com)

Dapper Labs partnered with the NBA to create NBA Top Shot, and its popularity among collectors has skyrocketed. Collectible moments such as videos, game highlights, photos, and art can be bought and sold on their dedicated marketplace. NBA Top Shot is an excellent marketplace for beginner NFT collectors who love basketball. Tearing open each digital pack is reminiscent of tearing open a physical pack of basketball trading cards, as you never know what you will get.

After purchasing a pack, you can sell it on the secondary market to turn a profit. You can buy moments using a debit or credit card and various cryptocurrencies. Collectors can also earn free NFTs by completing challenges or be eligible for free gifts. For example, I won a free Kevin Durant moment just by holding a minimum of 10 moments at the time of the event. The marketplace uses proof-of-stake to validate transactions since it is on the FLOW blockchain. This feature also makes it environmentally friendly, but you cannot transfer out your NFTs. Another downside is that there is a $25 fee to cash out a minimum of $30 from the marketplace.

Theta Drop (Website: thetadrop.com)

Theta Drop is a blockchain platform built to distribute videos and TV in a decentralized manner. The platform debuted in 2021 with the World Poker Tour's virtual collectible cards, containing moments of big plays during the tour. As an early adopter, the WPT used ThetaTV to stream content on the platform. To participate in this marketplace, however, you need to purchase THETA, also known as Theta Token (its native token). Various crypto exchange platforms, such as Binance, support THETA. Users can store the token in either Theta's crypto wallet application or an external crypto wallet, like Uphold. NFT creators need to apply for a drop on the platform and submit it for approval before a sale occurs.

Mintable (Website: mintable.app)

Mintable is a Singapore-based NFT marketplace backed by the billionaire Mark Cuban. Mintable aims to become a similar marketplace, if not greater than OpenSea, allowing you to browse, buy, and sell non-fungible tokens. The platform offers a variety of categories, including game items, collectibles, music, videos, utility, sports, and art. You must have ETH funds to make deals within their platform. To do so, you'll need a Metamask wallet. Mintable offers free and traditional minting, which requires gas fees according to the Ethereum Mainnet blockchain.

Nifty Gateway (Website: niftygateway.com)

Known to be a marketplace friendly to digital artists and musicians, the Nifty Gateway has facilitated the sale of famous digital artists like Beeple and even the singer Grimes. Powered by the Gemini crypto exchange, Nifties, the marketplace is built on Ethereum. As a result, you can purchase Nifties using fiat currency without first purchasing cryptocurrency. It is a very high-end marketplace that is exclusive to certain collectors. Creators must also apply and be properly vetted to sell on the platform. Although it is intuitive and easy to use, Nifty Gateway takes a 20% marketplace fee due to its exclusivity. The plus side, though, is that due to its custodial nature, transactions on the blockchain don't require gas fees, saving collectors the hassle and money upfront.

Foundation (Website: foundation.app)

As a simple, straightforward platform for bidding on digital art, since its design and launch in early 2021, Foundation.app has sold more than $100 million worth of NFTs (Ascent Staff, 2022). Built on the Ethereum blockchain, its simple interface has allowed many transactions within the platform. Buyers only need a crypto wallet with funds of ETH to begin purchasing. Foundation refers to itself as a "playground" for creators and collectors and encourages its users to connect their social media accounts. To sell your NFTs, community members need to upvote you, making it harder to sell NFTs on the platform. Although this feature upholds the quality of the work on the platform, it makes it challenging to create your own NFTs. Foundation.app probably isn't the marketplace you want to begin with, but you could revisit it once you have a following.

Atomic Hub (Website: atomichub.io)

Based on the WAX blockchain, Atomic Hub sets itself apart from other marketplaces that utilize ETH. Compared the Ethereum, WAX has small gas fees because it uses the proof-of-stake to validate transactions. This also makes it eco-friendly. Atomic Hub is known for selling NFT packs, which include collectibles of brands such as Funko, Topps Baseball cards, Garbage Pail Kids, Atari, Hasbro, and Mattel. Once opened, you can trade individual cards or collectibles on the secondary market. While users found creating an NFT complicated, Atomic Hub only takes a 2% fee on each NFT sale. Since this platform uses the WAX blockchain, you can't transfer your NFTs to the Ethereum network.

Magic Eden (Website: magiceden.io)

Magic Eden is an NFT marketplace that operates on the Solana blockchain. On Solana, transaction fees are a fraction of a cent, is lightning fast, and has less impact on the environment ("Magic Eden Playbook", n.d.). Phantom wallet and the $SOL token are primarily used on this platform. Users can mint NFTs using Magic Eden's launchpad or purchase NFTs directly from the secondary marketplace.

VeVe (Website: veve.me)

Veve is a mobile application you can download from Google Play or the App Store. Currently, VeVe only sells comic books, 3D collectibles, movie posters, tickets, and vehicles of famous brands and up-and-coming artists. VeVe has secured major brands such as Coca-

Cola, Disney, Marvel, Dreamworks, DC, and even the United States Postal Service. They claim that their collectibles are 99% environmentally friendly and are more efficient than Ethereum. You do not need cryptocurrency to buy NFTs, meaning you can use fiat currency to purchase collectibles through the app. You can, however, sell your NFTs within the app in exchange for Gems, just not for other forms of currency. One of the main downsides is the inability to transfer NFTs from within the VeVe app, but ECOMI, the company that owns VeVe, does plan to introduce this feature soon.

There are many other notable marketplaces out there, including Decentraland (decentraland.org), UFC Strike (ufcstrike.com), and Binance NFT (https://www.binance.com/en/nft/marketplace). Explore them all but go to their associated social media account to verify which is the correct website. Be careful. Many scammers create fake websites to lure people into stealing their information.

7

NON-FUNGIBLE GOODWILL

"You have not lived today until you have done something for someone who can never repay you."

— JOHN BUNYAN

G oodwill can be defined as an effort someone puts forth to help another out. When someone helps another person without expecting anything in return, they experience a sense of purpose, live a longer life, and achieve greater success. So, as you continue reading this book, as a goodwill gesture, I'd like to help you on your learning journey.

Would you take the time to help someone if it didn't cost you a dime? Your help would be invaluable and greatly appreciated. As someone who has been in your shoes and a beginner just like you, I was inexperienced and uninformed, but willing to learn. So, I did a lot of research and am now passing on this information to the world.

The only way to get this information to the public is to be seen, and reviews are a driving force in reaching our audience. If this book has proved to be valuable to you so far, would you take a minute right now to leave an honest review? Here is how your review will assist:

- It will help a future investor make an informed decision.
- It will help an entrepreneur support their family.
- It will change the way someone views NFTs and cryptocurrency.
- It will change how artists distribute their work.
- It will change someone's life for the better.

All you need to do is leave a review. Here's how…

If you are reading the e-book on **Kindle** or an e-reader, scroll to the end of the book, swipe up or to the left, and a prompt to "Review this book" will show. You can write a few sentences about the book and leave a star rating.

If you are listening to this on **Audible**, tap on the three dots at the top right of your phone or tablet and select "Rate & review." On your browser, select the title of the book and click on "More options" then "Write a review."

Or you can always go to the book page on **Amazon** or whatever platform on which you purchased this book, and leave an honest review. Your review is you; it is unique and one-of-a-kind and cannot be exchanged for another. So, thank you! **Just Visit the Link Below or Scan the QR Code !**

www.amazon.com/review/create-review?&asin= B0BMGT2MXL

If helping others you've never met brought a smile to your face, then that's awesome! You just offered a helping hand, and I'm thrilled to help you kickstart your investing journey.

8

CRYPTO WALLETS

WHAT ARE CRYPTO WALLETS?

Before you venture much further into the world of NFTs, you will need to consider a crypto wallet. A crypto wallet is a physical device or a software program that allows you to safely store your NFTs and cryptocurrencies and make crypto transactions. It consists of key pairs—the public and private keys.

A public key is an address you will use to send cryptocurrencies to the wallet. The most integral part of the wallet is the private key. Since this is like an actual password, new users can find themselves in trouble if they lose it. The private key serves much like the key to your safety deposit box. If someone gains access, they can access what is inside. Nevertheless, crypto users holding their private keys become their own bank, unlike renting a deposit box.

Joel Dietz, the founder of OneArt and contributing developer of MetaMask, defined a crypto wallet as the equivalent of a bank account (Nibley, 2021a). However, the main difference is that only you can access and control its contents if you have the key.

Many people still have little or no idea what cryptocurrency is; however, crypto wallets are user-friendly. Desktop wallets like Electrum and web wallets like MetaMask are built with a graphical user interface (GUI) designed for simplicity.

UNDERSTANDING HOW CRYPTO WALLETS WORK

As mentioned in the earlier chapters, a blockchain is a public ledger responsible for storing data in blocks. These record all transactions, wallet addresses, corresponding balances, and key holders that can access these balances.

Cryptocurrencies aren't stored in a wallet, per se. Those cryptocurrencies exist on the blockchain, and your wallet allows you access to those balances. The wallet enables holders to transfer their crypto anywhere. Likewise, it will allow others to see the balance in that address.

Generally, crypto wallets allow users to send, receive, and store cryptocurrencies like Ethereum (ETH), Binance (BNB), and Litecoin (LTC). Some also have a feature to buy and send cryptos, while others include additional features like swapping tokens and staking tokens for a fixed return paid out to users. It also allows access to decentralized applications (dApps) built on various networks.

While individual wallets have specific features, here are the basic steps to send or receive funds in a crypto wallet.

1. You must retrieve an address (or the public key) from your wallet to receive funds.
2. Find the "generate address" feature in your wallet and click to open.
3. Copy the alphanumeric address or QR code.
4. Share this with the person who will be sending you crypto.

To send funds, the process is much the same.

1. You will need the wallet address of the person you are sending crypto to.

2. Find the "SEND" function in your wallet and enter the recipient's wallet address.

3. Next, select the amount of crypto you will send and click. (Before sending a more considerable amount, consider sending a small test transaction.) Note that sending cryptocurrency requires a gas fee which you will pay the miners to process your transaction.

TYPES OF CRYPTO WALLETS

Crypto wallets are split into two categories: software and hardware.

Software Wallets

These desktop applications or browser extensions allow you to send, receive, and store cryptocurrencies. Software wallets keep your funds online and are called "hot wallets." There are a few types of software wallets.

▷ A Web-Based Wallet

An example of this is the MetaMask wallet. It works as a browser extension to send and receive ETH transactions to any wallet address. The browser extension makes it easy for you to interact with any DApp or DeFi protocol (Nibley, 2021). Metamask and Coinbase are examples of these type of wallets and can either be hosted or non-hosted.

▷ Desktop Wallets

The Exodus, Mycellium, and Ellectrum wallets are some examples of desktop wallets accessed via a laptop or computer. Typically, an anti-virus is needed to protect from threats that could harm or damage your computer software. Although they are secure and a great way to store crypto, it best to back up the computer frequently.

▷ Mobile Wallets

Mobile wallets allow users to store crypto and send or receive transactions all from the palm of your hands. In addition, instead of importing your crypto, you can sweep the private keys in an existing wallet by using a smartphone to scan the QR code. This will send all of your crypto or NFTs onto a whole new private key connected to the software wallet. Typically a small fee will need to be paid in order to do so. Some examples include Trust Wallet, Coinbase, Metamask, Alpha Wallet and Enjin Wallet.

In contrast to hardware wallets that often support multiple currencies, software wallets are unique to each currency. They can either be used on the web (custody wallets that aren't entirely secure) or in the form of an application installed on your laptop or phone where your private keys are stored. Because they're connected to the internet, they're less secure. Therefore, when using software wallets, make sure you have a backup. If issues arise in your browser or hard drive, you may lose your private keys, losing funds you cannot get back.

Hardware wallets

These are also known as "cold wallets" and serve a similar purpose but are physical devices you can plug into a computer and store crypto offline. Hardware wallets keep private keys that are in cold storage or held offline. This wallet is much more secure because you plug in the hardware wallet via USB port, and all signing happens offline. However, typical hardware is more complicated than a software wallet and costs around $50-$150 for the device. Some companies that make cold wallets include SafePal, Ledger, Trezor, and KeepKey, but be aware that not all are compatible with NFTs.

Hardware wallets interact with a computer through the following ways

- a separate software wallet
- a web-based interface
- a company-created application

If purchasing a hardwallet from an online store, be sure to check to see if it was tampered with in anyway. It is always best to purchase the device directly from the manufacturer to be safe.

Paper wallets

Paper wallets used to be a safe form of protection because they are not prone to attacks (Sharma, 2020). However, if someone gets a hold of your private key, you can kiss your crypto assets goodbye. This is why people shifted away from writing down their private keys on pieces of paper and found other ways of safeguarding their assets using other cold storage methods. It is still inadvisable to use this particular method unless you find a way to keep that piece of paper.

Depending on the user's goal, each type of cryptocurrency and NFT wallet has its use, although all accomplish the same purpose. Another way to store your private keys is through paper wallets.

HOW DO YOU CREATE A CRYPTOCURRENCY WALLET

Several crypto wallets currently exist, but the one that will suit you depends on how you use your cryptocurrency and the safety measures you want.

Hosted Wallets

The easiest way to begin is to set up a hosted wallet. When you purchase cryptocurrency via apps like Coinbase, the app automatically holds your crypto in a hosted wallet. (This means Coinbase is a third party that keeps your cryptocurrency for you.) The main benefit of using a hosted wallet is the safety of your cryptocurrency. However, it also has its drawbacks. With a hosted wallet, you can't access everything crypto has to offer; however, as hosted wallets develop more features, which will soon change.

1. **Choose a trusted platform.** You should consider ease of use, security of your funds or cryptocurrencies, and compliance with government and financial regulations.
2. **Create your account.** Provide your information and password. You may want to consider using two-step verification or 2FA for an extra layer of security.

3. **Buy or transfer crypto.** You may buy cryptocurrencies from a trading platform or exchange using your credit card bank account. If you already have some cryptocurrencies, you may share them with your hosted wallet for storage.

Self-Custody Wallets

Do you want to be in complete control of your cryptocurrencies? Using a self-custody wallet (or sometimes called a "non-custody" wallet) like the Coinbase wallet allows you to do so. As the name suggests, these don't need a custodian or a third party to keep your funds secured. While the platform provides you with the software to ensure the safety of your crypto storage, the responsibility of safeguarding it with a password lies with you. Losing your seed phrase or private key also means you can't access your funds. And if somebody else discovers your private key, they will have full access to your crypto, tokens, and NFTs.

Aside from controlling your crypto, you can also access more advanced crypto features like staking, yield farming, lending, borrowing, etc. But if your activities are limited to buying, selling, sending, and receiving. A hosted wallet could be the best option.

1. **Start by downloading a wallet app.**
2. **Create your account.** You are not required to provide your information or email address when setting up a non-custodial wallet.
3. **Write down your private key.** A private key is a random twelve-word phrase. Make sure that you keep it in a secure location. Losing it or forgetting it will result in losing access to your account.
4. **Transfer crypto to your wallet.** Purchasing crypto using fiat currencies like USD or Euros with a non-custodial wallet is not always possible. Therefore, you must transfer crypto into your non-custodial wallet from elsewhere.

If you are a Coinbase customer, you have two options. The *Coinbase app* is a hosted wallet where you can purchase and sell cryptocurrencies. Or you can choose to download the standalone *Coinbase Wallet app* if you want a non-custodial wallet. Those in the crypto and NFT space prefer to have both, so it is easy to buy cryptocurrencies with fiat currencies and participate in advanced crypto activities. Setting up any or both wallets is free of charge.

Hardware Wallets

These are the steps to set up a hardware wallet:

1. **Buy the hardware.** The two most popular brands are Trezor and Ledger.
2. **Install the software.** Depending on your chosen brand, download the system via the company's official website.
3. **Follow the instructions presented to create your wallet.**
4. **Transfer crypto to your wallet.** Like the non-custodial wallet, the hardware wallet won't allow you to buy crypto using fiat currencies, so you need to transfer crypto to your wallet from elsewhere.

Just as there are many ways to store cash in a bank account, there are also many ways to keep cryptocurrencies. If you want it simple, use a hosted wallet. A non-custodial wallet is better for complete control but use a hardware wallet for extra precautions. You can even have multiple types of wallets. With cryptocurrency, the choice is always yours.

GETTING STARTED WITH COINBASE

What You Will Need

If you are brand new to NFTs, you'll want to *create a Coinbase account* (n.d.) When setting up a crypto wallet , you will need to observe the following requirements:

- You must be at least 18 years old.
- You must have a government-issued photo ID (a passport is not allowed).
- You need a computer or smartphone that is internet accessible.
- You need a phone number connected to your smartphone.
- You must download the Coinbase app with an updated operating system or the latest web browser version.

Creating Your Account

1. You may download and open the Coinbase app on iOS or Android. However, Coinbase does not recommend access through your mobile device. To create your account, visit https://www.coinbase.com on your desktop browser.

2. Once you're on the website, you must provide the following information. The information you enter must be accurate and up to date to avoid any issues later.

    a. full legal name
    b. email address (one that is accessible)
    c. password
    d. your state (location)

3. Read and understand the "User Agreement and Privacy Policy."

4. Check the box **[Create Account]** when using a computer or click **[SIGN]** when using mobile to agree.

5. You'll receive a verification email from Coinbase sent to the email address you have provided.

6. When you get the verification email, click on the **[Verify Email Address]** button. Note that this email bears the address **no-reply @coinbase.com**. Clicking the link will redirect you to Coinbase.com.

7. Sign back in using the verified email and password to complete the email verification process.

Verify Your Phone Number

You will need the smartphone and phone number associated with your Coinbase account to complete a two-step phone verification process.

1. Start by signing in to Coinbase. Add your phone number.
2. Select the country where you live.
3. Enter the mobile number you're using.
4. Click [**Send Code**] for a computer or [**Continue**] for mobile.
5. Enter the **seven-digit code** you received in your phone number from Coinbase.
6. Click [**Submit**] or [**Continue**].
7. If you failed to receive the code, click [**Resend-SMS**].

Add Your Personal Information

You must enter the information shown on your valid government-issued photo ID. You'll need to submit a photo of this ID later.

- first name
- last name

- date of birth
- address

Provide answers for the following:

- For what purpose are you using Coinbase?
- What is the source of your funds?
- What is your current occupation?
- Who is your employer?
- What are the last four digits of your SSN?

After completing the application, you must wait for further instructions via email.

Verify Your Identity

1. Sign in to your Coinbase account.
2. Complete the ID verification process.
3. You'll want to protect your account from unauthorized access by setting up a two-step verification app (TOPP).

Link a Payment Method

To link a payment method, choose a country. This will let you know what payment methods are available in your location. After you connect a payment method, you can start buying and selling cryptocurrency.

HOW TO QUICKLY EARN $17 FOR FREE—NO STRINGS ATTACHED!

After opening an account on Coinbase, you'll have the opportunity to earn $17 worth of cryptocurrency at no cost to you. You don't need to buy anything first, nor do you have to deposit any money into your account. Here are just a few steps to get your money's worth from buying this book. Ready?

1. Login to your newly opened Coinbase account.
2. Click on "Learn and Earn" from the side menu.
3. Watch the lessons if you'd like or use the answer banks below for each cryptocurrency quiz.

AMP quiz answer bank (Earn $3 + $1 worth of AMP)

Earn $1 The Graph:

- Answer 1 - fully integrated apps and transformers

Earn $1 AMP per answer:

- Answer 1 - a collateral token
- Answer 2 - instant settlement assurance
- Answer 3 - AMP rewards

FETCH quiz answer bank (Earn $3 worth of FET)

Earn $1 FET per answer:

- Answer 1 - software agents that automate tasks
- Answer 2 - to power Fetch.ai agents
- Answer 3 - automated interactions with industries like travel and healthcare

Stellar Lumens quiz answer bank (Earn $10 worth of XLM)

Earn $2 XLM per Answer:

- Answer 1 - a decentralized protocol that unites the world's financial instruments
- Answer 2 - facilitating lost-cost universal payments
- Answer 3 - Transactions are fast, inexpensive, and global.
- Answer 4 - to issue, exchange, and transfer tokens quickly and efficiently
- Answer 5 - It relies on the cooperation of trusted nodes to confirm transactions.

You did it! You just earned $17 and are that much closer to investing in cryptocurrency and NFTs.

CRYPTO WALLET CONSIDERATIONS

When choosing a crypto wallet that best suits you, you need to consider the following:

- **How often do you trade?** How often you trade is essential when choosing a crypto wallet. Is it daily or only occasionally? Hot wallets are remarkable for their speed and practicality if you're an active trader. However, you may also benefit from using a cold wallet—like a savings account—just for safekeeping the bulk of your currencies.
- **What do you want to trade?** When buying crypto, are you interested only in Bitcoin, or do you want different types of cryptocurrencies? The crypto wallet you choose must support the currencies you wish to trade in both now and in the future.
- **How much are you willing to spend?** Do you plan to store a large amount of crypto? For this, a hardware wallet is most suitable. Still, unlike hot wallets, which are usually free of charge, hardware wallets require an upfront payment. Hot wallets are can be expensive and due to the higher trading fees and gas fees. However, the

advantage is that they offer faster transactions and greater functionality.

- **What functionality do you need in a wallet?** If you plan on doing something specific with crypto beyond trading, you should look for wallets that allow crypto lending, deposits, and staking.
- **Does it have an accessible interface?** If you're a beginner or a pro who's looking for a wallet, it would be best to consider a wallet that is accessible and has an intuitive user interface. Don't choose a wallet that is too complicated to work on when you're just starting your trading activity.
- **Does the wallet offer 24/7 customer support?** Having customer support available at all times is advantageous and beneficial for beginners. It is especially true as many wallets have visual glitches and bugs requiring frequent updates. You wouldn't want a wallet you can't depend on when encountering an issue.
- **Is the wallet compatible?** Are you serious about investing in crypto and NFTs? Consider getting a hardware wallet in addition to a software wallet. This is to ensure the safety of your digital assets. Choose a brand of hardware wallet compatible

with your software wallet since they can default to the model or models supported. You can transfer your cryptos back and forth as you need them.

Now that you've set up your wallet. Let's look into how to invest in NFTs.

9

A KICKSTART GUIDE TO INVESTING IN NFTS

NFTs were extremely popular during the pandemic, prompting many investors to ask how to get a hold of one. With the pixelated Crypto-Punk character images, artwork by Beeple, and Twitter CEO Jack Dorsey's inaugural tweet, many digital things have been auctioned as NFTs worth millions. As the value of cryptocurrencies rises, artists, collectors, and speculators are starting to flock to the NFT movement. No one knows whether this movement is the start of a new long-term investment or just a fad. But despite all these, NFTs show promise for artists, gamers, and entrepreneurs of the commercial world. They are an excellent option to expand your investment portfolio—with high risk and high returns.

Like a plot of land, NFTs cannot be reproduced and are one-of-a-kind. Because of this, you cannot exchange them for an asset bearing equal value, and they have no recognized market price. Additionally, NFT prices might rise or fall depending on their platform. Hence, they have no intrinsic value compared to paper money. NFTs are very new and are still subject to many changes and improvements and rules and regulations concerning profit models and copyright. Do your research before investing.

SHOULD YOU BUY NFTS?

The value of some NFTs has skyrocketed over the past year, attracting lots of attention from the investment community (Rossolillo, 2022). However, like any other investment, NFTs have upsides and downsides, which you should consider before buying them. Listed below are some of the pros and cons.

Pros

- The value of NFTs appreciates. Just as physical collectibles such as artwork and memorabilia go up in value, so do digital paintings, images, and videos.
- Buying and selling NFTs is more accessible nowadays. Unlike before, there is a lot of public

attention on NFTs, making it easier for them to be bought and sold.

- Creators and artists benefit from NFTs now more than ever. Aside from the publicity, creators and artists benefit from NFTs through royalties whenever someone purchases or resells them.

Cons

- Creating NFTs does not come without expense. Creating an NFT consumes a lot of time, work, and potentially money. The fees incurred can pile up and might become higher than the value of the NFT.
- Creating and verifying NFTs requires lots of energy. Aside from the physical energy needed to create the NFT, computers used to produce and verify NFTs consume a lot of electricity. This energy consumption drastically impacts our environment.
- Moreover, an NFT's value isn't permanent. Since they are non-fungible, NFTs might change in value depending on buyer demand. In other words, market volatility makes NFTs a high-risk investment.

ARE NFTS AN IDEAL INVESTMENT FOR YOU?

The NFT movement is still new, requiring much work and time to grow. Buying NFTs and understanding their value as a digital collectible could be considered a good investment, albeit speculative. Their monetary value is uncertain and will fluctuate depending on the demand.

There are no written rules to determine whether a certain NFT will rise or fall someday. However, identifying an NFT trend might pay off later if appropriately analyzed. After all, some digital artworks sold dirt cheap, eventually rose in value, and were resold for thousands of dollars years later. So, if you are an avid collector and have a good eye for things, investing in NFTs is a good idea.

STEPS TO INVEST IN NFT

Step# 1: Research Available NFTs

You want to pick an NFT which has a potential for value. There are elements that you need to consider, such as:

- the date of sale
- cryptocurrency requirements

- number of copies sold
- reputation of the team behind it
- on- or off-chain status (Avoid NFTs supported by off-chain. Most off-chain transactions use centralized servers, resulting in image loss if the servers go down.)

To get more information on a particular NFT, join the NFTs Discord and Telegram chats. You will learn more about the project and get a feel for what other NFT followers say.

Step #2: Select a Brokerage or Exchange When Purchasing Cryptocurrency

To purchase an NFT, you need to buy crypto. You can purchase most NFTs using Ethereum. You can buy Ether and other cryptos at a specialized crypto exchange or brokerages like Coinbase, Crypto.com, Gemini, Binance.US, or Kraken. Remember, a cryptocurrency exchange is an online platform where crypto trading takes place. At the same time, brokerages consist of individuals or firms serving as middlemen to facilitate the buying and selling of cryptocurrency.

When buying crypto, always remember that there are charges for transactions. Coinbase charges $0.99 for a trade of $10 or less, increasing as the trade amount increases. A SiFi investment charge is up to 1.25% of your crypto trade (Leonard, 2022). Fees can also be a flat fee per trade or a percentage of the thirty-day trading volume of an account. Take into consideration these charges to maximize the profitability of a trade.

Step #3: Select a Marketplace When Purchasing Your NFT

With this information, you can determine the scarcity of the NFT and choose one with future value potential, considering the law of supply and demand. You buy and sell NFT in the marketplace. Once you find the marketplace to sell your NFT, register and connect your crypto wallet to your account. Be aware that each marketplace has its own wallet requirements. There are two ways to sell your NFT items in the market—either through an auction or at a flat price.

Marketplaces that are popular today include the following:

- Axie Marketplace
- OpenSea
- Larva Labs
- Rarible
- NBA Top Shot Marketplace

When conducting a transaction, ensure you have enough crypto to cover fees. Fees may include the costs of buying and transferring cryptos, conversion, and gas fees. Remember that the listed price or the latest bid for an NFT item is not the total purchase price. You still must add the gas fee to arrive at the total purchase price of the NFT item.

FAQS

Are NFTs a Good Investment?

NFTs are still new, and like other cryptocurrencies, no one can say if they are a good investment because of their volatility. While they leverage blockchain technology, no one can know if they will retain their value in the long run. Therefore, anyone interested in investing in NFT should be cautious.

How Do NFTs Gain Value?

You can base the value of NFTs on these four significant factors

- **Future Value** involves speculations of users as to the direction of NFT over time.
- **Liquidity Premium** refers to the demand for the artwork, with higher traffic yielding higher premiums.
- **Utility** refers to how an NFT is used, such as a token in gaming.

- **Ownership History** refers to how NFTs play a role if the token is created by a famous brand or personality.

Can You Turn NFTs Into Cash?

Investors interested in digital collectibles are purchasing NFTs hoping that the item they bought today will make them a good profit in the future. You can sell NFTs in the marketplace for cash or cryptocurrency with all transactions recorded on the blockchain, ensuring ownership rights. Some marketplaces, such as VeVe, do not currently allow their users to cash out. So, many users are HODLing (holding on for dear life), hoping they can turn their profits into cash when that feature becomes available.

If you have decided to invest in NFTs, it's time to learn different ways on how to generate a stream of income from them.

10

INCOME WITH NFTS

Throughout 2021, the non-fungible token market has evolved into a significant part of the crypto business, with total spending on NFTs topping $12.6 billion, up from $162.4 million at the start of the year (Sergeenkov, 2022). While Ethereum is used to manufacture, buy, and sell most NFTs, hefty gas fees can make the process prohibitively expensive.

According to data retrieved from Rarible Analytics (n.d.) during the first quarter of 2022, minting a single NFT on Ethereum costs roughly $98.69 in gas expenses, while minting NFT collections costs around $900. To offset these expenses, many investors and developers simply try to sell their NFTs on secondary markets like OpenSea for a profit.

There are, however, ways to profit from NFTs other than selling them for more than you paid or developed them for.

PASSIVE INCOME

NFT Rentals

You can rent out your stock of NFTs, especially if they are in high demand. For example, some crypto games allow players to borrow in-game characters or items to increase their chance of earning tokens within the game ecosystem. Games like Townstar (via Gala Games) and Axie Infinity have NFTs that give users more earning potential and encourage the players to invest in them. Through the smart contract, the lender can set the terms of the rental agreement and the lease rate without fear of getting scammed or duped by the borrower. A really great example of this kind of platform is reNFT. They allow lenders to set borrowing periods, lease prices, and daily rates. Other platforms include Vera, IQ Protocol, and Trava NFT.

The reasons for renting an NFT vary for each person. People may want to rent NFTs because they wish only to use it for a limited time and cannot afford to purchase one. Some may have a desire to show off their social status, get early access to media content, or get access to events in venues that only allow a holder of a particular NFT entry.

NFT Royalties

One of the beauties of NFTs operating on blockchain technology is that it allows creators to set terms and impose royalty fees whenever their creation is sold on the secondary market. Trading on the secondary market generates passive income for creators and artists even after the NFT resells to various users. Using this strategy, they retain a share of the sales indefinitely. For example, if the royalty fee is set at 15%, the original creator will receive the same percentage each time their NFT gets sold to a new owner. Creators would need to set the royalty fee before minting their NFTs for this strategy to work.

Additionally, smart contracts govern the entire transaction and handle the distribution of royalties making everything fully automated. The creators do not need further intervention to implement their royalty terms or manually track down the payment due to the beauty of smart contracts.

NFT Yield Farming

Because of the infrastructures of decentralized finance (DeFi) and NFTs, it is now possible to provide liquidity to earn NFTs. For example, when you provide liquidity on Uniswap V3, the automated market marker (AMM) will issue an ERC-721 token or LP-NFT (LP stands for liquidity provider), which details your share of the total amount of those tokens in the liquidity pool. It also contains the pool's address as well as the symbol. Selling this NFT will further increase your position in the liquidity pools, generating more profits as time goes by.

Since NFTs are becoming a central element of automated market makers (AMM), users can use NFT-powered products to farm for yield. AMM users put their tokens into these formulaically price-determined pools. Yield farming leverages multiple DeFi protocols to generate the most significant allowable percentage yield using your digital assets (Sergeenkov, 2022). For example, the LP-NFTs issued on Uniswap can be staked elsewhere or used as collateral to bring in more yields. Doing so enables multiple income-generating streams for farmers.

Staking NFTs

One of the benefits of the DeFi and NFT partnership is that it makes it possible to stake NFTs. This means that they can be locked away using a DeFi protocol smart contract to generate yields or returns over time. Your NFT is offered as a reward or a staked token and provides liquidity and utility for a digital asset that is normally illiquid. Although some platforms support a wide variety of NFTs, others will require you to buy those which are native to their platform's utility token. Examples of these platforms are the NFTX, Only1, Splinterlands, Axie Infinity, and the Kira Network.

In some cases, these platforms give rewards in the form of governance tokens, which give holders voting rights on the platform's development of their ecosystems. An example of this is the Kingdom Warrior NFTs as well as the Slotie NFTs mentioned in Chapter 4. You can essentially earn money by holding onto an NFT. It is also possible to reinvest coins earned from staking NFTs into other yield-generating platforms.

ACTIVE INCOME

Selling NFTs on the Marketplace

An excellent and common way for people to earn money is by selling NFTs on the marketplace. As we looked at previously, here are some platforms and marketplaces where you can sell and trade your NFTs.

- Rarible
- OpenSea
- SuperRare
- Mintable

- NBA Top Shot
- And many more (for a breakdown of the most reputable ones, see Chapter 6)

NFT Sports Moments

The NFT market is opening great opportunities even in sports. These digital assets can be excellent income opportunities for sports like hockey, soccer, and baseball if applied correctly. They can help expand the fan base for each sport and provide enthusiasts with collectible memorabilia like jerseys, hats, and logos in digital format.

Like the gaming industry, sports need to adopt NFT technology as soon as possible to scale their market and provide a new way for fan engagement. A few organizations have done this and partnered with Dapper Labs, the team behind CryptoKitties, to create NFT moments, which are video based NFTs. NBA Top Shot has minted moments of many of the league's players, and UFC Strike likewise has NFT clips of their organization's fighters. NFTs can also include fans' favorite moments, historical videos, photos, etc. Selling the NFTs of packs you digitally tear open could earn you some income when sold on their respective marketplaces.

Licensed Collectibles

Aside from digital artwork, the most apparent application of NFTs is in the tokenizing of collectibles. Physical collectibles like action figures now have their digital equivalents. The VeVe marketplace has even secured Disney, Marvel, and Star Wars rights. Their goal is to create NFTs of famous characters and figures. Because NFT collectors are holding on to these for long periods, the rarest of these are highly valued and even more valuable than some of their physical counterparts.

NFT Video Games

Many expect that NFT-based video games could be the future of NFT technology. Unfortunately, until now, none of the games using NFTs have managed to gain widespread popularity. However, the potential of incorporating NFTs into video games is tremendous.

Gamers spend money on virtual in-game items, bringing billions to many platforms, including Call of Duty loot boxes, World of Warcraft gold, and Counter-Strike skins. If some video game companies were willing to sell in-game items as NFTs, it would surely be tremendous for the blockchain and gaming industries.

In-game NFTs are more advanced than simple digital trading cards or interactive NFTs like virtual works of art. Non-fungible tokens can be very complex and fully interactive when used in video games. They can also change over time, along with the player's character as you progress through the game.

It's worth noting that developers of video games that incorporate the use of NTS are among the most ambitious creators, and they might push the evolution of NFT forward.

By now, you may be wondering who can create NFTs. The truth is just about anyone can create one. All you need is a computer, internet access, and a little know-how. You'll learn how to do this in the next chapter.

11

CREATE, BUY, AND SELL NFTS

Here are step-by-step instructions to minting your first NFT, a popular platform for beginners called OpenSea. (There are other fantastic alternatives. Refer back to Chapter 6.)

CREATING NFTS

Step 1: Decide on a Concept

Every successful NFT release has a theme or a concept behind it. Whether a simple piece of art, or a complex story-driven set of characters, your NFT should mean something. The NFTs that do, tend to find a home in the wallets of prospective buyers.

Step 2: Decide on the Platform

Most people think you need advanced coding or programming skills when minting or creating NFTs. However, there are many platforms where non-technical beginners or first-time creators can mint their creations.

Platforms like OpenSea, Rarible, Holaplex, and Objkt are examples of platforms that are fundamentally user-friendly. However, note that each platform uses a particular blockchain and requires a specific wallet to use its services. For instance, OpenSea utilizes Ethereum and Polygon blockchains, and you need to have either a Meta-Mask or a CoinBase wallet. Holaplex, on the other hand, uses the Solana blockchain and requires you to have Phantom and Arconnect wallets. Also, remember that every platform demands creator and gas fees from its users for the platform to stay operational.

Step 3: Connect and Build a Community

One of the critical components of an NFT is the community that supports it and helps raise its monetary value. The more support a project gets from its community, the more famous it becomes, and its market value rises exponentially. So, if you are planning to mint NFTs, start using your Twitter account and join genre-exclusive platforms like Discord. That way, you can connect with people who will support your vision in the long run. Remember that your community will be the first to avail themselves of your NFT, so make sure you take good care of them. After all, a strong community of supporters is what gives NFTs value.

Step 4: Create Your Art

Whether it's music, artwork, poems, books, or in-game items, NFTs require a specific image to symbolize their existence. Be creative. Either use the tools you already have or invest in the technology to do so. Collaborate with other creators. With your audience in mind, decide whether you want your NFTs to have audio, video, or written elements in them. Be sure to figure out what kind of file type and file size the platform you are minting on requires (DeMatteo, 2022).

Step 5: Mint and Share

Depending on the platform, minting NFTs can be easy. For example, in OpenSea, it is as simple as uploading the files, writing a design description, creating the profile, determining royalty fees, and completing the listing. Once you mint the NFT, people can see it on your profile. Remember that blockchain is accessible by the public, so your NFT's transaction history will be recorded there forever.

SELLING YOUR NFT

If you want to start generating income, you need to sell your new NFTs. This can be done by promoting it to your community, maintaining the NFT supply, and monitoring the sales. You might also want to gradually lessen the supply as its value increases over time to induce scarcity.

BUYING NFTS ON OPENSEA

Step 1: Create a Wallet and Add Funds

To buy NFTs, you need a digital wallet and sufficient funds. Since Ethereum is the most commonly used on OpenSea, you can use the Coinbase Wallet since you've already created a Coinbase account. If not, you could use MetaMask—a popular web wallet for NFTs. Go to metamask.io, install it as a web browser extension, create a wallet, and link it to OpenSea. To do this, go to the top-right bar on OpenSea and choose a profile. You can select MetaMask from there. Grant OpenSea the necessary permissions to use the wallet and sign the signature request provided to you. Once done, you are ready to check out the NFT collections offered by the platform. Just click "Buy," give the necessary payment details to put some funds on your account, and you're good to go.

Step 2: Check Out the NFT Collections

To find the NFT you want to buy, go to your OpenSea profile and choose "Explore." From there, you will see the list of those available for purchase. You can narrow down your searches by clicking on specific tabs (i.e., trending, collectibles, music, photography, top art, and more).

Step 3: Purchase or Make Offers

Did a piece of CryptoArt or a GIF catch your eye? Well, you can buy it or make an offer to the sellers. You will also have an option to place a bid. Click on the button to make a purchase offer directly to the owner. You can check out the number of offers to know how much money you will need to bid on the item. However, remember that any bid on OpenSea should be five percent higher than the previous one.

Step 4: Check out the Purchase

Once you are ready to purchase your NFT, it will automatically take you to the checkout page. From there, you will see the details, such as the name, collection, subtotal, and the total after the fees incurred have been added. You will also see the amount you need to pay as a gas fee and the time required to process the transaction.

After you check out, the OpenSea will load up your MetaMask wallet. When you're all set to buy the NFT, confirm your purchase and wait until the platform processes the transaction. Once done, the NFT you purchased will appear in your collection.

SELLING YOUR NFT ON OPENSEA

If you decide to sell your NFTs via OpenSea, just hit "Sell" at the top-right bar. On the newly opened page, add in the necessary details and conditions of the sale. For example, choose whether to sell via auction, at a fixed price, or an offer option. You can also select the currency and expiration date for the sale. You can list your NFTs for free on the platform, but keep in mind that OpenSea charges up to 2.5% for each one sold (Oramas, 2022).

It is not as difficult to sell and buy NFTs as you might imagine. Just be aware that because of the popularity of NFTs and the crypto space in recent years, many scammers have jumped on the bandwagon and fraud is a concern. Because the market is relatively young, it does not yet have many regulations. Therefore, be very cautious and protect your investments and assets, as there are many risks and challenges in the NFT space.

12

POTENTIAL RISKS

I n previous chapters, we analyzed the immense potential of NFTs for digital content creators and collectors. But like with everything else in this space, there is also a downside. There are several challenges and risks associated with NFTs. They can bring in a lot of money to digital creators and marketplaces, which makes them a target for potential cyberattacks and fraud. Therefore, investing in NFTs can be risky. Before getting involved in NFT investing, consider the potential risks and challenges.

SMART CONTRACT RISKS AND MAINTENANCE OF NFTS

One of the main concerns in the NFT space is the risk of smart contracts and the difficulties of maintenance. In 2021, hackers attacked a well-known DeFi protocol called the Poly Network, a company that allows its users to swap tokens across different blockchains. The hackers stole a little over 600 million dollars' worth of assets (Parmar, 2022). The incident highlighted the vulnerability of the network's digital contracts and the ease of exploiting them.

Although almost half of the assets were returned to the network, the thefts perpetrated by the hackers demonstrated the risks associated with the NFT and DeFi sectors and the need for better regulation.

LEGAL CHALLENGES

We can't deny the rapid rise in the NFT market and the vast growth in how they are used. But with that comes a rising need for a regulatory body to keep up with the technological advancement. Because NFTs encompass various assets with unique traits, they are difficult to legally define in countries across the globe. Each country has a different way of classifying the different types of NFTs, and the laws that seek to regulate them cannot keep up with how fast this technology is advancing.

CYBER THREATS AND ONLINE FRAUD RISKS

With their growing popularity comes the possibility of cybersecurity threats and fraud in the NFT market. Common causes are copycat or fake NFT stores that set up shop and try to sell NFTs that are non-existent or counterfeit.

Another possibility is someone impersonating a famous artist to sell fake NFTs. The existence of copyright theft, fake giveaways, airdrops, and even replication of popular NFTs account for enormous fraud. Scammers even use social media to promote, advertise and coerce people into buying these imitation NFTs.

INTELLECTUAL PROPERTY RIGHTS

Issues with intellectual property rights also plague this market. Buyers are facing the issue of whether they actually own the right to the NFT they purchase. For example, when buying an NFT of a Marvel or Disney character from OpenSea or VeVe Digital Collectibles, you only have the right to use, display, and showcase the NFT you purchase. You will see the terms and conditions for the ownership of that specific NFT when you inspect the smart contract metadata. Intellectual property rights must be considered, including the right to publicity, copyrights, trademarks, and moral rights in respect of decentralized blockchain technology.

VALUATION CHALLENGES

Determining an NFT's value is a challenge. Factors that drive the NFT price are based on speculation. NFT valuation depends on its scarcity, perception, and on which platform it is distributed. It's hard to say how much a collectible is currently worth because it's based on how much someone wants to sell it and how much the other person is willing to pay. Because of this, the valuation of NFTs remains a big challenge, and prices fluctuate wildly.

NFTS AS SECURITIES CHALLENGES

Another challenge and risk facing NFTs are whether they are considered securities. The Security and Exchange Commission's (SEC) chairman, Gary Gensler, has investigated NFT creators and marketplaces to see whether they have committed any securities violations. Some of these infractions could be akin to selling fractional shares of NFTs as that could be considered a security. (Remember, fractional NFTs are when high-value NFTs are tokenized and traded as minor, more affordable pieces or fractions.) Unlike Bitcoin and Ethereum, NFTs are technically digital assets that can be sold for a profit and, therefore, could be classified as securities by the Howey test. Using the Howey definition, something is a security if it involves investors profiting from an asset in which they pooled their money together.

WHAT ARE THE EXPERTS SAYING ABOUT THE RISKS?

Volatility

According to Nadya Ivanova, COO of L'Atelier BNP Paribas, an emerging market research firm that published a report on NFTs in early 2021, the greatest strength of the technology surrounding NFTs is also one of its most significant weaknesses (Levin, 2021). Because anyone can create an NFT and post it on the internet, many poor-quality creations are being sold as NFTs and are flooding the market. Therefore, only those who have an eye for quality items can determine what is a good investment or a collector's item.

Ivanova sees the NFT market maturing and eventually becoming mainstream. Still, she recognizes the additional risks and unpredictability you should consider as an investor. Because there isn't any mechanism yet to help in pricing NFT assets, there is massive volatility in the market. In 2020 alone, the value of some popular NFTs catapulted by as much as 2000%, according to a published report. For example, some highlights on Top Shot which initially sold for a few dollars, spiked to tens of thousands.

Illiquidity

Liquidity is the ability of an asset to be easily exchanged for cash. An NFT's liquidity is more comparable to paintings or trading cards than stocks or crypto. This is because every seller must find a buyer willing to pay for a specific, unique item. It can put an investor in a tight spot if they spend a considerable amount purchasing an NFT and the market starts to tank. The holder of that NFT would be stuck with a digital asset they seemingly overpaid for.

On the other hand, Andrew Steinwold, a crypto investor, said that illiquidity has its upside. Steinwold started an NFT investment fund in 2019. According to him, if people don't panic and offload their NFTs, the market price of NFTs won't plummet (Levin, 2021). But, of course, this kind of panic selling typically would start such a sales frenzy.

Ownership

Steinwold explained further that those new to NFTs don't realize that there is usually a distinction between the token itself and the asset it refers to. The token is a record or proof of ownership residing on a blockchain. The asset the token refers to could be a GIF, JPEG, audio, or video file that is stored separately from the token.

Suppose a startup company that issued the NFTs decides to do a rug pull and stops hosting the digital artworks, trading cards, or cryptogames. In that case, buyers could be left with tokens that don't really point to anything because the NFTs no longer exist. There is a solution to this issue: storing files using decentralized services. This is now gaining traction.

For a professor of computer science at UC Berkeley, Nicholas Weaver, NFT ownership proves that tokens have no intrinsic value and that the frenzy surrounding them is as absurd as the Beanie Babies craze in the 90s (Levin, 2021). Beyond what a buyer is willing to offer, they hold no value whatsoever.

Foul Play and Fraud

Regardless of how impossible it is to pirate an NFT because each one is easy to track, people still try. Ivanova explained that anyone can mint a file and claim it is theirs. There is also manipulation that takes place in some markets. For example, wash trading is when an asset's price is artificially pumped up through opening multiple accounts and self-trading. This kind of manipulation can be detected by long-time collectors but may be difficult for beginners to notice.

Since blockchain transactions are immutable and anonymous, if someone gets hold of your private key to access your NFTs, tokens, or cryptocurrencies, you could lose it all. There's simply no getting them back. According to Weaver, the blockchain isn't the solution you are looking for when it comes to security.

Future Potential

Despite the risks and challenges in NFTs, Ivanova still sees enormous potential in the future. We can't avoid the correction, but the market will eventually continue to grow. There's the possibility that NFTs will become the underlying asset for an economy that takes place virtually within the Metaverse (see Bonus chapter).

Steinwold assumes that some people are just getting ahead of themselves. Still, he forecasts that NFT will grow to be a trillion-dollar market.

Weaver, the most skeptical of the three, believes that the current NFT hype is purely speculative and nothing but a bubble that will soon burst.

CAN THESE RISKS BE MITIGATED?

Cryptocurrencies are regulated when they are exchanged to reduce the risk of money laundering. We can likewise apply the same regulation to online auction houses for NFTs. Like financial institutions, compliant crypto exchanges, and the traditional art market, those companies wanting to conduct their business in the NFT space can implement a KYC (know your customer) system (Owen & Chase, 2021). This will help mitigate money laundering fraud.

In addition, NFT marketplaces can reduce these risks by implementing two-factor authentication for users and ensuring that their platform is safeguarded against hackers. Cyber security measures are needed as the digital world is prone to hacking.

Another way to mitigate risk is by creating a registry of stolen and fraudulent NFT purchases. The traditional art market already does this by listing stolen art and preventing them from being sold at auction houses in the real world. Some larger NFT auction house platforms already have these features to verify the creator claiming ownership of the token.

Because NFTs exist on blockchains renowned for their decentralized features, assigning a regulating body will undoubtedly lose its allure for users who want their transactions hidden from others' scrutiny. Also, once this is centralized, it will surely increase the processing cost and could pose more risk. Note that the more people involved in the process, the more it becomes subject to fraud and potential risks.

Before jumping on the bandwagon, it's essential to do your own research, especially when it involves digital assets like NFTs. Understanding the risks and challenges will help you make an informed decision rather than going with the hype. In addition, you can help mitigate the risks by remaining vigilant and careful, making investing in the NFT space easy.

13

NFTS AND TAXES

Whether you're an investor or an artist dealing with NFTs to generate profit, it is necessary to know and understand applicable taxes to avoid a sudden tax bill when the year ends. Any amount of wealth, regardless of what it is, can be taxed, especially if it has the potential to generate a stable source of income.

Amidst the hype and excitement about NFTs, most people ignore the taxation issue of every transaction around NFTs.

ARE NFTS TAXABLE?

In most cases, NFTs are subject to cryptocurrency laws determined by the country in which you live. For example, if you earn money from selling NFTs, you must report the proceeds as income when you file your income tax return (Fennimore, 2021). And if you decide to invest your money in NFTs, your digital assets will be subject to the capital gains tax. The most common taxable NFT activities include buying them with crypto, selling NFTs, and trading NFTs for other NFTs.

Taxes for NFT Creators

For NFT creators, the taxes imposed are straightforward. Even though creating NFT is not taxable, selling on platforms like OpenSea or Rarible is. The income you generate from selling your NFTs incurs taxes at the ordinary income tax rate, ranging from 10 to 37%. This is similar to getting paid after selling cryptocurrencies or mining. It is also subject to self-employment taxes of around 15.3% of total income.

Taxes for NFT Investors

For investors and traders of NFTs, you need to be aware of several taxable situations. Listed below are the typical instances wherein NFTs become taxable:

▷ Purchasing NFTs Using Fungible Tokens and Cryptocurrencies

Purchasing NFTs using cryptocurrencies like Ethereum incurs a capital gain or loss depending on the market. Depending on how long you hold your NFT purchase in the Ether, the transaction is subject to long-term or short-term capital gains tax rates. For example, if you buy NFTs using Ethereum on OpenSea or another marketplace, you must pay capital gains tax. However, if you purchased NFTs using depreciated Ether, you would incur a capital loss. You might get a chance to offset capital gains, effectively lowering your tax liability.

▷ Trading Your NFT for Another

NFT trading also triggers a taxable event. For example, if you buy an NFT worth $1,000 and exchange it for another NFT worth $4,000, the transaction will incur a taxable capital gain of three thousand dollars. The opposite is true if you trade down. You'll then incur a capital loss to offset your tax liability.

▷ Selling NFTs for Cryptocurrency

Selling NFTs incurs either a capital gain or loss depending on the market's movement. Hence, if you purchased an NFT worth $30,000 and then sold it later for $20,000, you would incur a capital loss of ten thousand dollars.

You Can Count on Gas Fees

Each time you sell or purchase an NFT, you'll have to pay a gas fee depending on what platform you use. Gas fees on Ethereum-based platforms, for example, are very costly. Whatever your purchase price for NFT during the transaction should be your basis of cost, including additional fees. If you were to purchase an NFT for $100 and sell it for $200, the capital gain would be $100. However, if you add the gas fee to the purchase price, your capital gains would only be $90 for purchasing that NFT. When you choose to sell the NFT, keeping track of the gas and additional fees will help reduce the taxes you will need to pay later.

Giveaways Are Taxable

Several projects within the community give away NFTs and fungible tokens using social media platforms. They are either airdropped or sent directly to your wallet if you win a challenge, comment on a post, or participate in the community's Discord channel. Giveaways, prizes, and rewards are taxable according to your standard tax rate. So, if you receive something for free from one of your favorite NFT projects, remember you could be taxed based on the equivalent dollar amount (DeMatteo, 2021). Although this is currently subjective since NFTs are volatile, you can use trends and records within the blockchain to estimate the value of each. If the NFT you received is widely known or is a blue-chip NFT, you can view the floor price at whatever trading platform sells them to determine the market value.

IRS AND NFTS

As of this writing, the US Internal Revenue Service has not yet taken a formal stance regarding the taxation of NFTs. However, it is possible that they will treat NFTs the way they treat cryptocurrencies, which are subject to capital gains tax that varies from zero to twenty percent depending on one's income. Alternatively, NFTs might be taxed higher if the IRS decides to treat those as collectibles, artworks, or trading cards, taxed at twenty-eight percent of one's monthly income. Whether they are rare collectibles or property, the difference will show if an individual holds the NFTs for over a year. Simply put, they will be subject to either capital gains or losses.

THE METAVERSE

WHAT IS THE METAVERSE?

B inance Academy (2021) defines the metaverse as, "a persistent, online 3D universe combining multiple virtual spaces, allowing users to meet, work, socialize, and play games in these 3D spaces." It's a digital simulation of the real world that integrates social media, blockchain technology, virtual reality (VR), augmented reality (AR), and other technologies to create an interactive place for users.

THE ORIGINS OF THE METAVERSE

You may think that the metaverse is a new concept or that you have become familiar with it after watching the movie *Ready Player One*. But the metaverse concept has been around for about 30 years, since Neal Stevenson introduced the term in the 1992 science fiction novel *Snow Crash* (XR Today Team, 2022). In it, users escape a futuristic and immensely anti-utopian world by entering the metaverse, a blending of the words *meta* (transcending) and *universe*.

For over three decades, many technological advancements have paved the way for the internet, online gaming, and virtual reality headsets. The popularity of all three mediums enabled people to use avatars within the game while trading in-game items, currency, and land.

The metaverse concept recently brought into the mainstream by Facebook rebranding as Meta will transform how we inhabit today's world. Facebook's Meta has several implications:

- Users will now occasionally inhabit an immersive reality in addition to the two-dimensional digital spaces.
- Designers—especially 3D modeling and VR world-building experts—and content creators can expect new opportunities in the future.
- It will open another economy where you can create, trade, and enhance wealth using related currencies different from those in today's world.
- New technologies have become necessary for the evolution of the metaverse.
- Real-world problems may take on a new dimension, but this time in a virtual one, such as concerns around security, data privacy, and ethical behavior.

HOW DOES CRYPTO FIT INTO THE METAVERSE?

Currently, video games offer the closest metaverse experience because of their emphasis on 3D virtual reality, but not just because of it. Video games now have features and services that cross over into different aspects of our lives. Take, for example, Roblox, which hosts virtual events like meetups and concerts. Players' activities in these games are no longer limited to playing games but have expanded to other activities and living their life in cyberspace.

Although gaming provides the 3D aspects of the metaverse, it does not cover every aspect of the virtual world that represents every aspect of our lives. We can say that cryptocurrencies integrate digital marketplaces and 3D virtual universes, including digital proof of ownership, governance, transfer of value, and accessibility, but what does this mean? If we're using the metaverse for purchasing virtual items in the future, we need to have a secure way to verify ownership. We also need to safely transfer these virtual items and money from one point to another. And finally, we also want to participate in the decision-making that will occur in the metaverse as it becomes a large part of our lives.

Today, some video games provide essential solutions to these issues, yet many developers opt for blockchain and crypto. While blockchain offers a transparent and decentralized way of dealing with topics, video-game development is more centralized. Video games, likewise, influence blockchain developers (Binance Academy, 2021). Gamification has become common in GameFi and Decentralized Finance (DeFi). These similarities will not end here and will only multiply as the two worlds integrate. The significant blockchain components that will be suitable for the metaverse are:

- **Digital Proof of Ownership:** Owning a digital wallet means you have access to your private keys. With these private keys, you can instantly prove your ownership of a digital asset or activity on a blockchain. Owning a wallet is one of the most secure ways of establishing identity and proof of ownership.
- **Digital Collectability:** A metaverse must look for ways to incorporate real-life activities. While you can prove your ownership of an item, you can likewise prove its originality and uniqueness. Through NFTs, you can create images and unique things that others can't forge or replicate, and a blockchain can represent ownership of these items.
- **Transfer of Value:** The metaverse must find a way to transfer value that users can trust. Many know that in-game currencies are less secure than cryptocurrencies on a blockchain. So, if people spend more time and money in the metaverse, they will need a reliable currency.
- **Governance:** Metaverse users will also be concerned about the ability to control the rules

of interaction. In real life, members have voting rights to elect leaders either in private companies or in the government. The metaverse needs to find a way to best implement fair governance, and blockchains revolutionized this.

- **Accessibility:** Creating a digital wallet on a blockchain is simple and can be done by anyone. Unlike bank regulations, you don't need to provide personal information or pay anything. Because of this, the blockchain is considered one of the most accessible methods to manage your finances and online identity.

- **Interoperability:** The blockchain is continuously improving its compatibility with other platforms. For example, Avalanche (AVAX) and Polkadot (DOT) allow the creation of custom blockchains that can interact with each other. A single metaverse needs to connect with multiple platforms.

METAVERSE EXAMPLES

In the absence of a single, linked metaverse, we have several platforms and projects similar to a metaverse, commonly incorporating NFTs and blockchain elements. Here are some examples:

Axie Infinity

This game is designed to provide a consistent earning opportunity for players in developing countries. By owning three creatures known as Axies, you can start farming the Smooth Love Potion (SLP) token. You can either purchase Axies or receive them as gifts. At the time of writing this, Axies sell for anywhere between $200 to $1,000. Their value fluctuates depending on the market price, and your earning potential depends on your play time. Although Axie Infinity does not give users the ability to select or change their avatars, it does give players a quasi-job within the metaverse. Many Filipinos, for example, have been using Axie Infinity as an alternative way to earn a living.

Second Life

Second Life is a three-dimensional virtual environment using avatars for education, business, and mingling. It is a community where you can express yourself by selling and buying clothes to customize your avatar. This metaverse-like environment has an NFT marketplace for trading collectibles with others.

Decentraland

Decentraland is an online digital ecology where players actively participate in the platform's governance. Decentraland established a complex crypto economy by combining social elements with NFTs, cryptocurrencies, and virtual real estate. Players use NFTs to represent cosmetic collectibles and the MANA cryptocurrency to purchase 16x16 land parcels.

WEB 3.0 VS. THE METAVERSE: WHAT'S THE DIFFERENCE?

If there's one thing that needs to evolve constantly, it's the internet. This is because a large part of the world's population relies on the internet in many different aspects of their lives—from social to business to entertainment. If you're curious about the internet of the future, you have most likely encountered the terms *metaverse* and *Web 3.0*. You'll notice that these two are not actually the same thing (Houser, 2022).

What is Web 3.0?

Web 3.0 is rooted in the idea that a significant shift in how we use the internet has already occurred. This shift pulls us away from Web 1.0 (the internet of the past) to Web 2.0 (the internet of the present).

Web 1.0 operated between 1991 and 2004 (Wildfire, 2021). If you needed information immediately, you could find it on the world wide web. However, at this point in internet history, the volume of content created could not meet the need for that content.

The introduction of Web 2.0 defined the version of the internet dominated by user-created content. At this point, people started to interact through social media posts on Facebook and sharing YouTube videos. Users could leave comments anywhere and everywhere across the internet.

Today, many are speculating how Web 3.0 will look or function. Gavin Wood, the co-creator of the Ethereum blockchain, predicted as early as 2014 that the future internet would be blockchain-centered (Edelman, 2021).

The core idea behind the created design of blockchain technology is its decentralized character. So, instead of storing data on central servers owned by one entity, an entire network of computers owned by several individuals with a unified copy of the information can replace it using blockchain technology. Monetarily speaking, it's the difference between a network of computers keeping track of every transaction on a shared ledger and one bank tracking your account activity on the server it owns.

However, financial transactions are just one of the many applications for blockchain networks. They may also serve as storage for all kinds of data. If the proponents of Web 3.0 have their way, blockchains will serve as the foundation of the internet of the future.

NFTs and Decentralized Web Browsers: Early Signs of Web 3.0

You're witnessing the gradual emergence of Web 3.0 as people get involved with NFTs, which use blockchain technology to help artists distribute and monetize their digital creations. Another example is decentralized web browsers, such as Brave, which allow users to choose which sites can access their browsing information. Brave can also block ads and users earn tokens simply by using their browser.

The Connection Between Web 3.0 and the Metaverse

Web 3.0 and metaverse technologies support each perfectly. Although Web 3.0 favors a decentralized internet, it still has the potential to serve as an excellent hub for connectivity inside the metaverse. An example of where these two technologies could integrate is when a digital artist might consider creating a unique pair of sneakers for an avatar to wear in the metaverse. They can then sell an NFT and provide the buyer sole (pun intended) rights to own the shoe. The owner can then flex by using their avatar and prove that they have exclusive ownership if someone tries to create a copy of the shoe.

Can the Metaverse Transform How We Work, Socialize, and More Online?

Suppose the tech industry cannot overcome current hardware limitations. In that case, we may end up accessing Web 3.0 through computers and smartphones instead of VR headsets. Intel predicted that computers must be one thousand times more efficient to support the metaverse. There hasn't been a company to offer a comfortable but affordable VR headset at this point.

If the plans for the metaverse come to fruition, it could be a mixture of both—centralized and decentralized. For example, when Facebook named its project "Meta," this strongly indicated its intention to build and monetize the metaverse—the exact thing Web 3.0 aims to prevent from happening. However, there are metaverses like Decentraland where everything in it is created and belongs to its users.

The Web 3.0 experience could offer users a new way to derive income from digital assets listed for sale in the metaverse. But it may also pave the way for massive corporations to view it simply as a way to get even richer.

So, while we now catch glimpses of metaverse and Web 3.0, neither is willing to divert from today's method of accessing the internet—a screen-based approach in which competing centralized corporations currently occupy.

Founder of Twitter, Jack Dorsey, declared that a decentralized internet wouldn't increase users' power as proponents of Web 3.0 predict but will instead remove that power from big tech and place it in the palms of venture capitalists investing in blockchain apps. For Jack, Web 3.0 will ultimately be a centralized entity, just with a different label (Kastrenakes, 2021).

People may still prefer their current interaction with the internet even if technological barriers to building the metaverse are solved. Even Elon Musk, the proponent of cutting-edge technology and CEO of Space X and Tesla, said he couldn't picture someone "strapping a frickin screen" to their faces all day (Tech Desk, 2021). Therefore, a screen-based internet that incorporates new Web 3.0 and metaverse aspects is the most likely future for the internet.

FUTURE OF THE METAVERSE

Facebook has been promoting a unified metaverse which is particularly interesting for a social media network with an enormous market base. Mark Zuckerberg has made it clear that he intends to create a metaverse project to promote remote labor and expand financial prospects for citizens of developing nations. It will change the future of work

Facebook's enormous market base and ownership of communication, social media, and crypto stage provide the metaverse with an excellent place to start by integrating all of these into a unified system. Other technology giants like Microsoft, Google, and Apple are also considering the creation of a metaverse.

When considering a metaverse powered by cryptocurrencies, combining a place to buy and sell NFTs along with VR is the next best move. NFT holders can sell their items on multiple marketplaces like Rarible and OpenSea. However, for the 3D platform, nothing like this is available. Some blockchain developers might consider developing popular quasi-metaverse applications with more loyal users rather than one large tech company.

Although it may seem like we are still a long way from creating a single, cohesive metaverse, we are already beginning to see signs of change that could bring this concept to fruition. It is unknown if we'll ever be able to achieve this feat, but in the meantime, we have projects that allow us to virtually experience a virtual life in a virtual world.

CONCLUSION

Now that you have finished reading this book, we hope you understand the general phenomenon of NFTs, blockchain, cryptocurrency, and the metaverse.

You have learned how to evaluate risks and begin investing in NFTs, and you've learned how to mint, buy, and sell NFTs for profit while keeping in mind the taxes you will owe. We have also looked at the basics of blockchain technology, and cryptocurrencies. Finally, we looked at the possibilities of the metaverse.

Learning about digital assets, bitcoin technology, and the metaverse before diving into the NFT investment pool will guide you through your investing journey and towards success. This knowledge will be handy, especially for beginners investing in blockchain, NFTs, or other cryptocurrencies.

Despite being fully armed with all the necessary information required to succeed in investing, you still need to be cautious as NFTs are still in their infancy.

So, based on the information provided in this guide, it is time for you to make an informed decision when choosing to join this new but futuristic wave of digital collectibles.

If, in any way, you feel that you have benefited from reading this book, leave a review so that the correct information can reach millions of other potential digital asset owners.

Just Visit the Link Below or Scan the QR Code!

www.amazon.com/review/create-review?&asin=
B0BMGT2MXL

REFERENCES

Akamo, A. (2022, March 3). Why the us sec is investigating nfts. *Nairametrics.* https://nairametrics.com/2022/03/03/the-us-sec-is-investigating-the-nft-market-over-potential-securities-violations/

AlexWGomezz. (n.d.). *Nft smart contracts explained.* Cyber Scrilla. https://cyberscrilla.com/nft-smart-contracts-explained/

Ascent Staff. (2022, January 5). *10 best nft marketplaces | the ascent by motley fool.* The Motley Fool. https://www.fool.com/the-ascent/cryptocurrency/nft-marketplaces/

Ashford, K. (2020, November 20). *What is cryptocurrency?* Forbes Advisor. https://www.forbes.com/advisor/investing/cryptocurrency/what-is-cryptocurrency/

Authors, G. (2021, October 23). *NFTs for freedom: Nonfungible tokens and the right to self-determination.* Cointelegraph. https://cointelegraph.com/news/nfts-for-freedom-nonfungible-tokens-and-the-right-to-self-determination

Baggetta, M. (2021, October 4). *What is crypto mining? How cryptocurrency mining works.* Blockgeeks. https://blockgeeks.com/guides/what-is-crypto-mining/

Bailey, J. (2018, January 19). *What is cryptoart?* Artnome. https://www.artnome.com/news/2018/1/14/what-is-cryptoart

Bhagat, V. (2022, April 11). *Pros and cons of blockchain technology: Your complete go-to guide.* PixelCrayons. https://www.pixelcrayons.com/blog/pros-and-cons-of-blockchain-technology-your-complete-go-to-guide/

Binance Academy. (2021, September 21). *What is the metaverse?* https://academy.binance.com/en/articles/what-is-the-metaverse

Binance Academy. (2022, March 30). *Blockchain advantages and disadvantages.* https://academy.binance.com/en/articles/positives-and-negatives-of-blockchain

Bogna, J. (2022, January 8). *What is the environmental impact of cryptocur-*

rency? PCMAG. https://www.pcmag.com/how-to/what-is-the-envi ronmental-impact-of-cryptocurrency

Brooks, B. (2021, October 28). *Facebook Changes Company Name to Meta, Plans NFT Support.* Crypto Briefing. https://cryptobriefing.com/ facebook-changes-company-name-to-meta-plans-nft-support/

Chan, K., & O'Brien, M. (2021, April 20). *Q&A: Artist Beeple on selling NFT collage for a record $70M.* AP NEWS. https://apnews.com/arti cle/beeple-interview-nft-digital-art-sold-70-million-364d9a574dc32d7bbb83e1a81c7ac913

Crane, C. (2020, October 16). *What is crypto mining? How cryptocurrency mining works.* InfoSec Insights. https://sectigostore.com/blog/what-is-crypto-mining-how-cryptocurrency-mining-works/

Charles X. (2021, January 11). *Top 10 nft marketplace to launch your nft and own the best.* Finextra. https://www.finextra.com/blogposting/ 21563/top-10-nft-marketplace-to-launch-your-nft-and-own-the-best

Create a coinbase account. (n.d.). Coinbase. https://help.coinbase.com/ en/coinbase/getting-started/getting-started-with-coinbase/create-a-coinbase-account

DeMatteo, M. (2021, December 16). *The top 5 tax tips for nft investors.* https://www.coindesk.com/markets/2021/12/16/the-top-5-tax-tips-for-nft-investors/

DeMatteo, M. (2022, January 24). *Minting your first nft: A beginner's guide to creating an nft.* https://www.coindesk.com/learn/minting-your-first-nft-a-beginners-guide-to-creating-an-nft/

Duggan, W. (2022, May 31). *What is ethereum 2. 0? Understanding the merge.* Forbes Advisor. https://www.forbes.com/advisor/investing/ cryptocurrency/ethereum-2/

Earn staking rewards on Coinbase. (n.d.). Coinbase. https://www.coin base.com/staking

Edelman, G. (2021, November 29). *The father of web3 wants you to trust less.* Wired. https://www.wired.com/story/web3-gavin-wood-interview/

Tech Desk. (2021, December 23). *Elon Musk mocks 'Metaverse' idea, says nobody wants a screen strapped to their face.* The Indian Express.

https://indianexpress.com/article/technology/tech-news-technol
ogy/elon-musk-mocks-metaverse-idea-says-nobody-wants-a-
screen-strapped-to-their-face-7686834/

Esajian, P. (2022, June 1). *How to invest in nfts: The beginner's guide (2022).* FortuneBuilders. https://www.fortunebuilders.com/how-to-invest-in-nfts/

Evm explained - what is ethereum virtual machine?. (2021, July 23). Moralis. https://moralis.io/evm-explained-what-is-ethereum-virtual-machine/

Fennimore, E. (2021, June 9). *Nft tax guide: What creators and investors need to know about nft taxes.* Taxbit. https://taxbit.com/blog/nft-tax-guide-what-creators-and-investors-need-to-know-about-nft-taxes

Frizzo-Barker, J., Chow-White, P. A., Adams, P. R., Mentanko, J., Ha, D., & Green, S. (2020). Blockchain as a disruptive technology for business: A systematic review. *International Journal of Information Management, 51,* 102029. https://doi.org/10.1016/j.ijinfomgt.2019.10.014

GaryVee. (2021). *What is nft? Non-fungible token guide.* Gary Vaynerchuk. https://www.garyvaynerchuk.com/what-is-nft-non-fungible-token-guide/

Hong, E. (2022, May 5). *How does bitcoin mining work?* Investopedia. https://www.investopedia.com/tech/how-does-bitcoin-mining-work/

Houser, K. (2022, January 21). *Web 3.0 vs. the metaverse: What's the difference?* Freethink. https://www.freethink.com/technology/web-3-vs-metaverse

Iredale, G. (2020, November 3). *History of blockchain technology.* 101 Blockchains. https://101blockchains.com/history-of-blockchain-timeline/

John, L. (2021, September 21). *How to create a cryptocurrency wallet?* ReadWrite. https://readwrite.com/how-to-create-a-cryptocurrency-wallet/

Kastrenakes, J. (2021a, March 1). *Grimes sold $6 million worth of digital art as NFTs.* The Verge. https://www.theverge.com/2021/3/1/22308075/grimes-nft-6-million-sales-nifty-gateway-warnymph

Kastrenakes, J. (2021b, December 21). *Jack Dorsey says VCs really own Web3 (And web3 boosters are pretty mad about it)*. The Verge. https://www.theverge.com/2021/12/21/22848162/jack-dorsey-web3-criti cism-a16z-ownership-venture-capital-twitter

Kay, G. (2021, March 20). *We talked to crypto-art investors to figure out what's driving people to spend millions on NFTs, despite no guarantee their value will increase*. Business Insider. https://www.businessin sider.in/tech/news/we-talked-to-crypto-art-investors-to-figure-out-whats-driving-people-to-spend-millions-on-nfts-despite-no-guarantee-their-value-will-increase/articleshow/81605087.cms

Kesonpat, N. (2020, October 10). *Creators, communities, and the gray space in the middle*. Nichanan Kesonpat. https://www.nichanank.com/blog/2020/10/9/gray-space-in-the-middle

Kingdom Warriors (n.d.) https://kingdomwarriorsnft.com/mint

Leonard, K. (2022, May 20). *How to invest in nfts: 3 steps (Video) | seeking alpha*. Seeking Alpha. https://seekingalpha.com/article/4471296-how-to-invest-nft

Levin, T. (2021, March 13). *NFTs could be the future of collecting—Or a huge bubble. We talked to 3 experts about the risks to consider before buying in*. Business Insider. https://www.businessinsider.in/tech/news/nfts-could-be-the-future-of-collecting-or-a-huge-bubble-we-talked-to-3-experts-about-the-risks-to-consider-before-buying-in-/articleshow/81485561.cms

Leyes, K. (2021, December 27). *3 ways to make money with non-fungible tokens (Nfts)*. Entrepreneur. https://www.entrepreneur.com/article/368122

Magic Eden Playbook (n.d.). *Intro to nfts on solana*. Magic Eden. https://contenthub.magiceden.io/playbook

Market Trends. (2022, January 25). *What is NFT and how to earn with it*. Analytics Insight. https://www.analyticsinsight.net/what-is-nft-and-how-to-earn-with-it/

Natively Digital: A Curated NFT Sale/Lot 2. (N.d.). Sotheby's. https://www.sothebys.com/en/buy/auction/2021/natively-digital-a-curated-nft-sale-2/quantum

Nayak, C. (2022, February 9). *Tech InDepth: Understanding crypto mining*

and its ups & downs. The Indian Express. https://indianexpress.com/
article/technology/tech-news-technology/tech-indepth-under
standing-crypto-mining-and-its-ups-downs-7764321/

Neti (2022, April 12). Blockchain Platforms 2022. *Medium.* https://
medium.com/@neti-soft/blockchain-platforms-2022-
662171d0b3b7

NetworkNewsWire. (2020, June 23). *The new gold rush isn't gold.* https://
www.prnewswire.com/news-releases/the-new-gold-rush-isnt-
gold-301081595.html

NFTs and Crypto, what's the difference? (2021, December 8). Defiance
ETFs. https://www.defianceetfs.com/nfts-and-crypto-whats-the-
difference/

Nibley, B. (2021a, October 28). *What is a crypto wallet? Understanding the
software that allows you to store and transfer crypto securely.* Business
Insider. https://www.businessinsider.in/investment/news/what-is-
a-crypto-wallet-understanding-the-software-that-allows-you-to-
store-and-transfer-crypto-securely/articleshow/87341592.cms

Nibley, B. (2021b, November 4). *What is the ethereum virtual machine
(Evm)?* SoFi. https://www.sofi.com/learn/content/what-is-
ethereum-virtual-machine/

Non-fungible tokens (Nft). (n.d.). Ethereum.Org. https://ethereum.org

Non-fungible tokens—Risks and challenges. (2021, September 14). *101
Blockchains.* https://101blockchains.com/nft-risks-and-challenges/

Oramas, J. (2022, January 13). *How to buy and sell your first nft on
opensea? A step-by-step guide.* CryptoPotato. https://cryptopotato.
com/how-to-buy-and-sell-your-first-nft-on-opensea-a-step-by-
step-guide/

Owen, A., & Chase, I. (2021, December 2). *Nfts: A new frontier for money
laundering?* Rusi. https://rusi.org/explore-our-research/publica
tions/commentary/nfts-new-frontier-money-laundering/

Parmar, D. (2022, February 22). *Challenges and risks associated with non-
fungible tokens (NFT).* Geekflare. https://geekflare.com/finance/
nfts-challenges-and-risks/

Perspectives, O. by A. S., Flora Harley for CNN Business. (2021, April
2). *Opinion: NFTs: Fad or future? 2 experts weigh in.* CNN. https://

www.cnn.com/2021/04/02/perspectives/nfts-blockchain-technol
ogy-fad-future/index.html

Rarible Analytics. (n.d.). *Live from rarible.* Retrieved on March 9, 2022,
from https://raribleanalytics.com/

Rea, A. (2021, March 3). *Non-fungible tokens: 101.* Sylo. https://medium.
com/sylo-io/non-fungible-tokens-101-31d144cbc229

Rodriguez, G. (2022, August 5). *7 best crypto wallets of august 2022.*
Money. https://money.com/best-crypto-wallets/

Rosenberg, E. (2022, June 30). *How does bitcoin mining work?* The
Balance. https://www.thebalance.com/how-does-bitcoin-mining-
work-5088328

Rossolillo, N. (2022, June 29). *How to buy and sell nfts.* The Motley Fool.
https://www.fool.com/investing/stock-market/market-sectors/
financials/non-fungible-tokens/how-to-buy-nft/

Sergeenkov, A. (2022, March 9). *5 ways to earn passive income from nfts.*
https://www.coindesk.com/learn/5-ways-to-earn-passive-income-
from-nfts/

Sharma, T. (2020, July 2). *Types of crypto wallets explained | blockchain
council.* https://www.blockchain-council.org/blockchain/types-of-
crypto-wallets-explained/

Smart contracts explained - what are smart contracts?. (2021, July 2).
Moralis. https://moralis.io/evm-explained-what-is-ethereum-
virtual-machine/

Steinwold, A. (2019, October 7). *The History of Non-Fungible Tokens
(NFTs).* Medium. https://medium.com/@Andrew.Steinwold/the-
history-of-non-fungible-tokens-nfts-f362ca57ae10

Steinwold, A. (2020, June 19). *Crypto will change value, nfts will
change society.* Zima Red. https://andrewsteinwold.substack.com/p/
crypto-will-change-value-nfts-will

Tang, N. (2021, April 12.). *The ethereum virtual machine: How does it
work?.* Phemex. https://phemex.com/academy/ethereum-virtual-
machine

Tenorio, E. (2021, June 29). *Advantages and disadvantages of blockchain.*
BBVA. https://www.bbva.ch/en/news/advantages-and-disadvan
tages-of-blockchain/

Thomas, L. (2022, May 26). *A guide to cryptopunks nfts: Pricing, how to buy, and more.* Nft Now. https://nftnow.com/guides/cryptopunks-guide/

Upgrading ethereum to radical new heights. (n.d.). Ethereum. https://ethereum.org/en/upgrades/

Voigt, K., & Rosen, A. (2022, June 13). *Cryptocurrency: What it is and how it works.* NerdWallet. https://www.nerdwallet.com/article/investing/cryptocurrency

What is blockchain technology? How does it work? (2022, July 28). Built In. https://builtin.com/blockchain

What is cryptocurrency? (n.d.). Coinbase. https://www.coinbase.com/learn/crypto-basics/what-is-cryptocurrency

Why nft art is becoming so popular. (2021, June 3). Fabriik. https://fabriik.com/threads-of-thought/why-nft-art-is-becoming-so-popular/

Wildfire. (2021, March 17). *History of digital marketing: how do we remember the web.* https://www.wild-fire.co.uk/history-of-digital-marketing-how-we-remember-the-web/

Wilson, T., Westbrook, T., & John, A. (2021, August 11). *Hackers return $260 mln to cryptocurrency platform after massive theft.* Reuters. https://www.reuters.com/technology/defi-platform-poly-network-reports-hacking-loses-estimated-600-million-2021-08-11/

Wolfson, R. (2018, January 9). *How a hackathon birthed the CryptoKitties origin story.* Bitcoin Magazine. https://bitcoinmagazine.com/markets/how-hackathon-birthed-cryptokitties-origin-story1

Wong, B. (2021, July 27). *The history of nfts & how they got started.* Portion Blog. https://blog.portion.io/the-history-of-nfts-how-they-got-started/

XR Today Team. (2022, January 10). *Metaverse meaning—What is this new world everyone's talking about?* XR Today. https://www.xrtoday.com/mixed-reality/metaverse-meaning/

Printed in Great Britain
by Amazon